ÇA MARCHE !

JUNIOR CYCLE FIRST YEAR FRENCH

1

MARIA HARNEY

g GILL EDUCATION

Gill Education
Hume Avenue
Park West
Dublin 12
www.gilleducation.ie

Gill Education is an imprint of M.H. Gill & Co.

© Maria Harney 2017

ISBN: 978-0-7171-72283

Design and origination: Littlebug Graphic Design

Illustrator: Sarah Wimperis

Cover designer: Graham Thew

At the time of going to press, all web addresses were active and contained information relevant to the topics in this book. Gill Education does not, however, accept responsibility for the content or views contained on these websites. Content, views and addresses may change beyond the publisher or author's control. Students should always be supervised when reviewing websites.

The author and publisher have made every effort to trace all copyright holders, but if any have been inadvertently overlooked we would be pleased to make the necessary arrangement at the first opportunity.

For permission to reproduce photographs, the author(s) and publisher gratefully acknowledge the following:
© Alamy: 2BR, 14 (Gerard Butler, Michael D. Higgins, Kate Middleton, Angela Merkel, François Hollande, Justin Bieber, Juliet Binoche, Robert Lewandowski), 15 (Niall Horan, Nicola Sturgeon, Gerard Piqué, Kanye West, Taylor Swift, Katie Taylor), 19TR, 20 (6), 20 (7), 29C, 30TR, 54TR, 68C, 68BL, 69TR, 79 (Champs-Élysées), 84 (4), 106TL, 169 (French jam, Cornflakes), 185 (Nutella), 203C, 204TR, 240 (Marion Cotillard, Omar Sy, Audrey Tautou), 260B (12). © Getty Images: 77BR, 79TR. © iStock: 1CL, 2TR (3), 2 (Louis Pasteur), 3 (5), 4 (5), 5, 6BR, 7 (3), 10, 12TR, 14 (8 flags), 18 (6), 19 (6), 20 (2), 21BR, 22 (7), 28C, 28TR, 28BL, 29 (2), 32 (6), 33 (4), 34 (2), 35 (3), 36BR, 37TR, 38 (2), 40BR, 41 (6), 42 (2), 43 (4), 44 (7), 46TL, 47C, 48BR, 51TR, 63 (3), 64TR, 67CR, 70 (2), 71CR, 72BR, 73TR, 74TR, 75BR, 76BR, 77TR, 77 (Barack Obama, SpongeBob Squarepants), 78 (5), 79TL, CR, CL, BR, 80BR, 81TR, 82 (8), 83C, 86 (4), 91 (4), 92TR, 93 (6), 94TR, 96BR, 97TR, 102 (2), 104 (6), 105B, 106TR, CR, BR, 107C, 108CR, 109TR, 112 (3), 114 TC,TR,CR, 115 (3), 116TL, 129 (5), 130TR (2), 132TR, CR, 134 (4), 136 (2), 137C, 138 (3), 139 (5), 141 (2), 144BR, 145BL, 146CR, 148 (9), 150CR, 153 (2), 154 (6), 156TR, 157 (4), 158 (10), 160 (15), 162TR, 167 (4), 169 (9), 170 (8), 171 (4), 175BR, 176BR, 177TR, 180CR, 181 (7), 182TR, 184TR, 185 (11), 186CR, 188TR, 190BR, 191 (8), 192CR, 193TR, 203 (4), 204B (8), 206 (2), 211 (3), 217BR, 221 (2), 229 (5), 231 (2), 234 (12), 247B (4), 248B (2), 256 (6), 258 (11), 259 (8), 260TR (4). © Rex: 77 (Ron Weasley). © Topfoto: 22 (Harry Potter).

Acknowledgements

A very special thank you to my family, for all your love and support. Je vous aime.
A tremendous team worked tirelessly to produce this beautiful, fun and exciting language course, many thanks to all at Gill Education and Dog's-ear, especially to Margaret and Emma.

Table des matières

OH-LA-LA

Unité	Statement of Learning (SOL) and Strand (S)	Vocabulaire	Grammaire
Unité 1 **Je me présente**	**SOL: 2, 6, 16, 24** **S1: Communicative Competence** 1.1, 1.2, 1.3, 1.6, 1.7, 1.9, 1.10, 1.11, 1.12, 1.13, 1.14, 1.17, 1.18, 1.21 **S2: Language Awareness** 2.1, 2.3, 2.4, 2.5, 2.6, 2.7 **S3: Socio-cultural Awareness** 3.1, 3.2, 3.3, 3.4, 3.8	Je me présente p.6 Tu as quel âge ? p.12 Les nombres de 1 à 15 p.12 Un poème p.13 Les nationalités p.14 À mon avis p.20	Mots transparents p.4 Faux amis p.4 Tu ou Vous p.5 Les adjectifs p.6 Les noms p.18 L'article défini p.18
Unité 2 **Au collège**	**SOL: 2, 6, 16, 24** **S1:** 1.1, 1.2, 1.3, 1.5, 1.6, 1.7, 1.9, 1.10, 1.11, 1.12, 1.13, 1.14, 1.16, 1.17, 1.21, 1.22 **S2:** 2. 1, 2.3, 2.4, 2.5, 2.6, 2.7 **S3:** 3.1, 3.2, 3.4, 3.9	Bonne Rentrée p.28 Dans la salle de classe p.31 Mes affaires d'écoles p.42 Parlons en classe p.48 L'alphabet en français p.51 Les jours de la semaine p.52	Les verbes et les pronoms sujets p.35 Le pronom *on* p.36 Le verbe être p.37 L'article indéfini p.40 Qu'est-ce que c'est ? – C'est/ Ce sont p.42 La négation p.47
Unités 1 et 2 **À vous de jouer !**	**SOL: 2, 6, 16, 24** **S1:** 1.5, 1.6, 1.7, 1.9, 1.10, 1.11, 1.12, 1.13, 1.14, 1.15, 1.17 **S2:** 2.1, 2.2, 2.3, 2.4, 2.5 **S3:** 3.1, 3.2, 3.3, 3.3, 3.4	Lisez p.57 Civilisation p.57 Grammaire p.57 Écrivez p.58 Grammaire p.58 Écrivez p.59 Jeu de plateau p.60 Une petite pièce de théâtre p.62	
Unité 3 **Ma famille, mes animaux et moi**	**SOL: 2, 6, 16, 24** **S1:** 1.2, 1.3, 1.5, 1.6, 1.7, 1.9, 1.10, 1.11, 1.13, 1.14, 1.15, 1.17, 1.18, 1.19 **S2:** 2.1, 2.2, 2.4, 2.5, 2.6, 2.7 **S3:** 3.2, 3.4, 3.8	Ma famille p.64 Je parle de ma famille p.70 Les descriptions p.73 Les mois p.78 As-tu un animal de compagnie chez toi ? p.82	Un verbe irrégulier – avoir p.66 Les adjectifs p.75 L'adjectif possessif p.79 Les adjectifs – la place et l'accord p.83

|

Unité	Statement of Learning (SOL) and Strand (S)	Vocabulaire	Grammaire
Unité 4 **Chez moi**	**SOL: 2, 6, 16, 24** **S1:** 1.1, 1.2, 1.3, 1.6, 1.7, 1.8, 1.9, 1.10, 1.11, 1.13, 1.14, 1.15,1.17, 1.18, 1.19 **S2:** 2.1, 2.2, 2.4, 2.5, 2.6, 2.7 **S3:** 2.2, 2.4, 2.8	Tu habites où ? p.92 Dans ma maison, il y a… p.95 Un poème p.99 Les nombres 16 à 30 p.100 Les tâches ménagères p.103 Les points cardinaux p.106	Des prépositions p.92 Il y a/ il n'y a pas p.96 Les verbes –er p.111
Unités 3 et 4 **À vous de jouer !**	**SOL: 2, 6, 16, 24** **S1:** 1.5, 1.6, 1.7, 1.8, 1.9, 1.10, 1.11, 1.12, 1.13, 1.14, 1.15, 1.161.17, 1.18, 1.19, 1.20, 1.22 **S2:** 2.1, 2.2, 2.4, 2.5 **S3:** 3.1, 3.2, 3.3, 3.6, 3.10	Lisez p.121 Civilisation p.121 Grammaire p.122 Écrivez p.125 Jeu de plateau p.126 Une petite pièce de théâtre p.128	
Unité 5 **Mon temps libre**	**SOL: 2, 6, 16, 24** **S1:** 1.1, 1.2, 1.3, 1.5, 1.6, 1.7, 1.8, 1.9, 1.10, 1.11, 1.12, 1.13, 1.14, 1.15, 1.16, 1.17, 1.18, 1.19, 1.20, 1.22 **S2:** 2.1, 2.2, 2.4, 2.5, 2.6, 2.7 **S3:** 3.1, 3.3, 3.6, 3.7, 3.10	Les sports p.130 Des sports individuels p.136 Les installations sportives p.141 Quand est-ce que tu joues au foot ? p.141 Depuis quand est-ce que tu fais de la gymnastique ? p.145 Les passetemps p.148 Les saisons p.157 Quel temps fait-il ? p.158	Jouer à p.133 Le verbe *faire* et les sports p.137 Depuis p.144 Les verbes en –ir p.150 Un verbe irrégulier –aller p.155 en/au et les saisons p.157
Unité 6 **À table**	**SOL: 2, 6, 16, 24** **S1:** 1.1, 1.2, 1.3, 1.4, 1.5, 1.6, 1.7, 1.9, 1.101.11, 1.12, 1.13, 1.14, 1.15, 1.16, 1.17, 1.18, 1.19, 1.20, 1.22 **S2:** 2.1, 2.2, 2.4, 2.5, 2.6, 2.7 **S3:** 3.1, 3.3, 3.7, 3.9, 3.10	Le petit déjeuner p.169 Le déjeuner p.170 Le diner p.171 Les dessert p.171 Les quantités p.172 Chez un glacier p.185 Les nombres de 30 à 100 p.189	Le verbe manger p.174 Le verbe boire p.174 L'article partitif p.176 La préposition au, à la, aux, à l' p.184 Je voudrais p.187 Les verbes en –re p.192

Unité	Statement of Learning (SOL) and Strand (S)	Vocabulaire	Grammaire
Unités 5 et 6 **À vous de jouer !**	**SOL: 2, 6, 16, 24** **S1:** 1.5, 1.6, 1.7, 1.8, 1.9, 1.10, 1.11, 1.13, 1.14, 1.15, 1.16, 1.17, 1.18, 1.19, 1.20, 1.22, **S2:** 2.1, 2.2, 2.4, 2.5 **S3:** 3.1, 3.2, 3.3, 3.4, 3.6, 3.10	Lisez p.199 Civilisation p.199 Grammaire p.199 Écrivez p.199 Jeu de plateau p.200 Une petite pièce de théâtre p.202	
Unité 7 **Une journée au collège**	**SOL: 2, 6, 16, 24** **S1:** 1.1, 1.2, 1.3, 1.5, 1.6, 1.7, 1.9, 1.10, 1.11, 1.12, 1.13, 1.14, 1.15, 1.17, 1.18, 1.19, 1.20, 1.22 **S2:** 2.1, 2.2, 2.4, 2.5, 2.6, 2.7 **S3:** 3.1, 3.3, 3.4, 3.7, 3.10	Mon collège et ses équipements p.204 Les matières p.208 Mes opinions p.210 Ill est quelle heure ? p.213 Une journée typique p.219	Plus … que or Moins … que p.211 Les verbes pronominaux p.220
Unité 8 **Les vacances**	**SOL: 2, 6, 16, 24** **S1:** 1.1, 1.2, 1.4, 1.5, 1.6, 1.7, 1.8, 1.9, 1.10, 1.11, 1.12, 1.13, 1.14, 1.15, 1.17, 1.18, 1.20, 1.22, **S2:** 2.1, 2.2, 2.4, 2.5, 2.6, 2.7 **S3:** 3.1, 3.2, 3.3, 3.7, 3.8, 3.9	Mes vêtements p.237 Les affaires indispensables en vacances p.242 A l'aéroport – Les panneaux p.244 Shopping à l'aéroport p.246 Tu vas où ? p.247 Tu loges où ? p.247 Une carte postale p.250 Au terrain de camping p.251 Les animaux du parc d'animalier p.258 Une journée dans un parc d'attractions p.260	Je vais en/au/aux p.230 Tu voyages comment pour aller en vacances ? p.231 Je voudrais p.233 Le verbe faire p.236 Le verbe prendre p.236 Le verbe porter p.239 Le futur proche p.254
Unités 7 et 8 **À vous de jouer !**	**SOL: 2, 6, 16, 24** **S1:** 1.5, 1.6, 1.8, 1.9, 1.10, 1.11, 1.12, 1.13, 1.14, 1.15, 1.16, 1.17, 1.18, 1.19, 1.20, 1.22 **S2:** 2.1, 2.2, 2.4, 2.5 **S3:** 3.1, 3.2, 3.3, 3.4, 3.5, 3.6	Lisez p.266 Civilisation p.267 Grammaire p.267 Écrivez p.267 Jeu de plateau p.268 Une petite pièce de théâtre p.270	

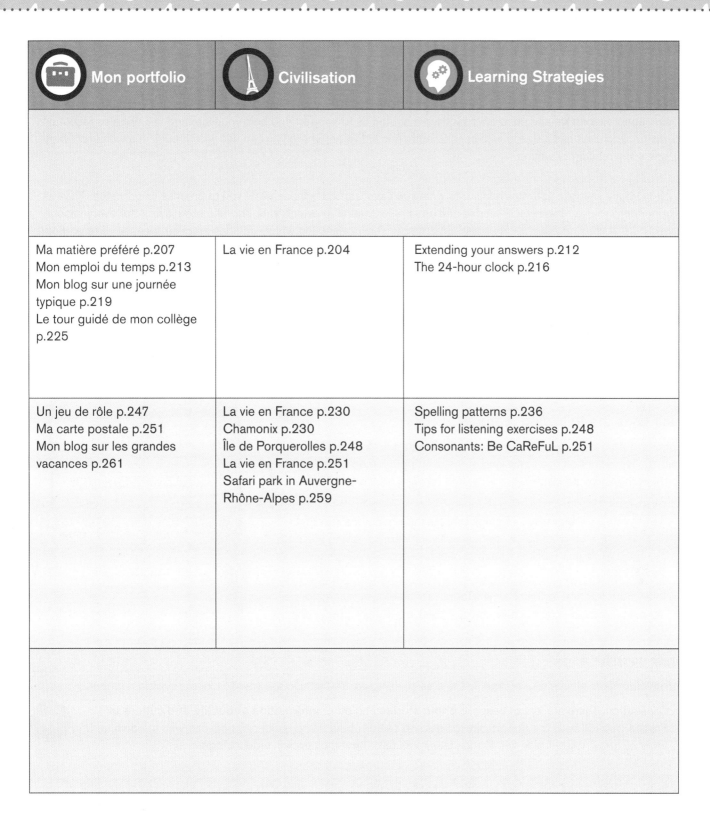 Mon portfolio	Civilisation	Learning Strategies

Introduction: Welcome to *Ça Marche !*

Ça Marche ! 1 is an engaging, fun, creative textbook and suite of resources which will guide you on your French language journey. You will learn the French language and have opportunities to use it in authentic situations relevant to modern life. You will learn about French life and culture, you will learn strategies to support and help you learn and you will also reflect on your experience. Each unit has a theme with specific authentic activities, where you can use your French in a variety of ways–listening, speaking, reading or writing.

In each unit there are portfolio activities relating to what you have learned – these allow you to practise your French. There is also the opportunity to use different ICT modes and oral presentations to extend your portfolio exercises. After every second unit you will find – *A vous de jouer !* – *Your turn/Give it a go!* This is a section which includes practice exercises and games that you can play in class, as well as small dramas which you can have fun acting out.

The approach used throughout *Ça Marche ! 1*, is 'Assessment for Learning (AfL)', so you are constantly supported in your learning. Success criteria ensure you have specific guidelines for your portfolio pieces, self and peer assessment ensures you have detailed and specific feedback to inform your next step, *Astuces* provide strategies, along with discussion activities to ensure you understand new language points. Innovation, creativity, activity, engagement, authenticity and communication are central to each unit and the activities you will participate in. Like its title suggests, *Ça Marche ! 1* works for your learning in every way.

Each unit uses the following features:

Unité opening page: Listed here is what **you will be able to do** by the end of the unit. You will reflect on this at the end of the unit through **'can do' statements in the** Bilan de l'Unité.

Objectifs: Language **targets** throughout the text that you can use to self-assess your learning, giving you and your teacher a snap shot of how you are progressing.

Draw the face in the box next to the objective that best reflects your learning.

- The happy face means you are fully confident and know this learning point.

- The neutral face means you are still not fully confident, and may either need to revise the learning point or ask your teacher to explain it again.

- The unhappy face means you are finding the area challenging. You should ask your teacher to explain it further.

 Civilisation: There are lots of bespoke **photo stories** and other **information about life and culture in France**. You will have the opportunity to hear and see all about it and make comparisons with our own and other cultures. You will also see French teenagers talk about their lives in **video blogs**.

 Mots-clés: The **keywords** you will meet and use throughout each unit. They are also summarised at the end of every unit (**Récapitulatif**), in one handy spot when you need to revise.

 Astuces: Tips and **learning strategies** to help you as much as possible as you learn French.

 ICT: Weblinks where you can find games, activities, famous French places, songs and lots of other fun French information at the click of the mouse in the eBook – or by typing the web address into your search bar.

À deux: Oral activities where you get to **speak French with a partner**, asking and answering questions based on the topics in each unit.

 Interévaluation: Peer assessment, where you **give your partner detailed feedback** based on criteria in your book. These are a great help and support for you and your classmates: you will have specific feedback to go on based on your peer assessment.

 Participez: Learning activities such as **think-pair-share and group work,** where you discuss and practise explaining the rules behind grammar points.

 Mon portfolio: You will see this icon when you need to complete an exercise in your portfolio. There, you are given **an exercise with specific success criteria** (a checklist to ensure you do well!). You then self-assess from a list of *étoiles* (stars) and *voeux* (wishes) where you decide what you deserve a star for, and what areas you wish to improve on in your next exercise.

Mon brouillon (My draft): A prompt in the portfolio to write and reference a **draft** of your work.

Mon bilan d'apprentissage (My Learning Assessment): A **reflection** exercise you complete at the end of your portfolio pieces, which keeps you focused and makes sure that you are organised and managing your work, as well as your learning.

 This section is a review at the end of each unit that includes a summary of keywords, a checklist of learning and a reflection section.

 Mots-clés: A **summary of the key vocabulary** and verbs you meet in each unit. This is a very handy section when it comes to revision – everything is in one spot.

 Bilan de l'Unité: A **checklist** of what you should be able to do by the end of a unit. It allows you to see where you are doing really well, and what areas you might still need to revise or get some help with.

 Discutez en classe: An opportunity for you, with your classmates, to look back over the unit, see what you enjoyed or didn't enjoy, what you found helpful and what your aims are for the next unit. It is a way to **plan and manage your learning**.

Some other icons you will meet:

 Écoutez/*Listen*   Écrivez/*Write*   Lisez/*Read*   Parlez/*Speak*   Grammaire/*Grammar*

As well as your portfolio booklet, there are also 2 audio CDs which come free with this book as well as a **FREE interactive eBook**, where you can access the videos and photo stories.

I hope you enjoy your journey with the French language and *Ça Marche ! 1* will ensure it works out perfectly for you!

Bonne chance !

The teacher's resource pack includes a ***Teacher's Resource Book,*** which provides lots of extra support and resources for each unite in the *Ça Marche ! 1* textbook.

UNITÉ 1

Je me présente

PARIS

La Seine

Strasbourg

Loire

Dijon

Massif central

Chamonix

Dordogne

Alpes

Bordeaux

Rhône

Pyrénées

Nice

Marseille

OH-LA-LA

By the end of this unit you will

- Know a little about France and its influences on our life and language
- Understand how languages spoken by other people in your class can help you to learn French
- Understand how to greet a person in French
- Be able to introduce yourself in French and ask questions about another person
- Be able to count from 1 to 15 in French
- Know some French gestures and idioms
- Know about nouns and the definite article
- Be able to say what you like, and give your opinion in a group.

Ex. 1.1 La Vie en France

Regardez la video et répondez aux questions en anglais. *Watch the video and answer the questions in English.*

What do you know about France and the French language? You may actually know quite a lot already! Can you answer these questions?

1. What is the capital of France?
2. What is the population of France (approximately)?
3. Name three French foods.
4. Name three French sports.
5. Name three French landmarks.
6. What is the symbol of France?
7. What does the French flag look like?

Search for 'French national anthem' on YouTube to hear '*La Marseillaise*'.

Every day we encounter French influences on our lives, without even realising it!

- Food
- Cars
- Travel
- Medicine

Having good French is a huge asset when it comes to finding a job.

Many celebrities speak French. Research online and try to find five famous people who speak French.

Astuces

Many of us already have experience of different languages at home or at school. Are there any students in your class whose first language is not English? Your native language, the one you learned as a baby, is called Language 1; your second language is Language 2, and so on. A person who has learned a second language has a lot of experience in thinking about words, spellings, sounds and pronunciation. Ask your classmates if they can share any advice or tips on learning Language 2!

Ex. 1.2 Sondage en classe

1. What languages are spoken in your class? _____

2. What is the highest number of languages spoken by a student in your class? _____

3. For each of the languages spoken in your class, what are the words for *hello* and *goodbye*?

_____

 European Day of Languages is held on 26 September every year. Search for 'European Day of Languages' on **www.leargas.ie** and plan a project for your class or school.

 Objectifs

- I can say hello and goodbye in more than two languages
- I can give at least one tip to help learn a new language
- I can give some facts about France

 Mon portfolio 1.1: Mon passeport pour les langues

Faites cet exercice dans votre portfolio. *Do this exercise in your portfolio.*

gr There are quite a few English words in the French language. These are called **cognates**: words that look and/or sound similar and mean similar things in English and in French. Look at the words below. How many of them do you already know? Can you add to the list?

Ex. 1.3 Mots transparents

Lisez ces mots transparents. Vous les comprenez ? *Read the cognates below. How much French do you already know?*

Écoutez le CD et entrainez-vous à bien prononcer le vocabulaire.
Listen to the CD and repeat the vocabulary to improve your pronunciation.

- le tennis
- le ballet
- le restaurant
- le grand prix
- le weekend

- la cuisine
- le hamburger
- le croissant
- le sport
- la musique

- les bonbons
- la télé
- les tomates
- les carottes

Prononciation

When learning new French words, remember these basic pronunciation tips.

1. The last consonant of French words is usually not pronounced. But some such as *c, r, f,* and *l* are pronounced. So be **CaReFuL!**

2. If a word is long, break it into syllables and give each syllable the same amount of stress.

3. The French *r* sound comes from the back of your throat.

4. Try to sound French, just like the people you hear on the CD that comes with this book!

Do this, even if you are learning a new word and are not sure of the exact pronunciation: if you try to say it with a French accent, it will sound a lot better!

Faux amis means *false friends*. These are French words that look and/or sound like English words but have different meanings. For example: *collège*. This does not mean *college*, but *secondary school*. It corresponds with our 1st to 3rd year. Another example is *les baskets*: it does not mean *baskets* – it means *runners*!

Objectifs

- I can explain what cognates and *faux amis* are

When French people meet, they greet each other with one kiss on each cheek. Sometimes family members or good friends will kiss more than once on each cheek. But *faire la bise* is for friends and family. When meeting strangers or acquaintances in a business or more formal setting, French people will shake hands like we do.

Tutoyer et vouvoyer

There are two words for *you* in French: *tu* and *vous*.

We use *tu* for friends, family and people we know very well.

We use *vous* in a more formal way, for adults and people we don't know. *Vous* is called 'you formal'. It is also 'you plural', so when we want to say *you* to a group, we use *vous*.

Ex. 1.4 Tu ou Vous ?

Il faut dire *tu* ou *vous* ? *Discuss the following situations and decide whether you would use* tu *or* vous.

1. Speaking to your friend in school

2. Speaking to your teacher

3. Asking someone for directions in the street

4. Speaking to a group of French teenagers

Objectifs

- I can use *tu* and *vous* in the right situations

Ex. 1.5 Vocabulaire

Écoutez le CD et entrainez-vous à bien prononcer le vocabulaire. *Listen to the CD and repeat the vocabulary to improve your pronunciation.*

- Bonjour
- Je te présente ...
- Ça va ?
- Merci
- Salut
- Voici
- Ça va, et toi ?

Ex. 1.6 Vocabulaire

Écoutez le CD et entrainez-vous à bien prononcer le vocabulaire. *Listen to the CD and repeat the vocabulary to improve your pronunciation.*

Sophie : Bonjour Emma, je te présente Audrey. Audrey, voici Emma.	**Emma :** Salut, Audrey ! Ça va ?
	Audrey et Emma : Oui, merci. Et toi ?
Audrey : Salut, Emma !	**Sophie :** Ça va, merci.

Ex. 1.7 Les présentations

En groupe de trois, faites les présentations sur le modèle de Sophie, Audrey et Emma. *In groups of three, introduce two of your friends to each other, like Sophie does for Audrey and Emma in Ex. 1.6.*

Ex. 1.8 Vocabulaire

Écoutez le CD et entraînez-vous à bien prononcer le vocabulaire. *Listen to the CD and repeat the vocabulary to improve your pronunciation.*

Je me présente

- Bonjour
- Salut
- Coucou
- Au revoir
- Ça va ?
- Ça va bien, merci.
- Non, ça ne va pas très bien.

- Comme-ci comme-ça
- Et toi ?
- Moi aussi, ça va ! / Moi non plus, ça ne va pas.
- Comment tu t'appelles ?
- Je m'appelle …
- Tu habites où ?

- J'habite à Dublin.
- Tu as quel âge ?
- J'ai douze/treize ans.
- Je suis irlandais/irlandaise, indien/indienne, britannique, etc.

Adjectifs. *Adjectives.*

These are describing words, such as:

irlandais/irlandaise, indien/indienne, britannique.

Adjectives in French have different spellings depending on whether the person they are describing is masculine or feminine.

The general rule is to add *e* to adjectives to make them feminine.

There are some exceptions, e.g. *indien/indienne*, which adds an extra *n* and *britannique* which stays the same.

We will learn more about adjectives later in this unit and further on in the book.

Prononciation

Intonation

When asking a question in French, we raise our voices at the end of the sentence. Practise this with your classmates, using the questions above.

Ex. 1.9 Lisez

Lisez la conversation et répondez aux questions. *Read the conversation and answer the questions.*

Jean : Bonjour.	**Jean :** Je m'appelle Jean. Ça va ?	**Jean :** J'habite à Galway. Et toi ?
David : Salut.	**David :** Ça va bien. Et toi, Jean ?	**David :** J'habite à Clare.
Jean : Comment tu t'appelles ?	**Jean :** Moi aussi ça va, merci.	
David : Je m'appelle David. Et toi ?	**David :** Tu habites où ?	

1. How does Jean say hello?

2. How does David greet Jean?

3. Can you say the following out loud?

   - Tu habites où ?

   - Comment tu t'appelles ?

4. Write your own answers to the following questions in French:

   - Ça va ? _____

   - Comment tu t'appelles ? _____

   - Tu habites où ? _____

5. Where does Jean live?

6. Where does David live?

7. Match each sentence with the correct answer.

Comment tu t'appelles ?	Ça va bien, merci.
Tu as quel âge ?	Je m'appelle Michael.
Tu habites où ?	J'ai 12 ans.
Ça va ?	Salut, Antoine.
Voici Antoine.	J'habite à Rennes.

Astuces

If the question is asked in French, answer in French!

If the question is asked in English, answer in English!

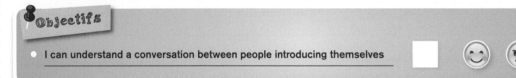

Ex. 1.10 Le blog vidéo «Je me présente»

Regardez le blog vidéo. Répondez aux questions en anglais. *Watch the video blog and answer the questions in English.*

1. What is the girl's name?

2. How old is she?

3. Where does she live?

4. What is the name of her school?

5. She likes football. True or false?

Objectifs

- I can understand a conversation between people introducing themselves   🙂 😐 🙁

Ex. 1.11 À deux

À deux : posez les questions à votre camarade et répondez à ses questions. Complétez la grille. *Talk with your classmate. Ask them questions and reply to theirs. Fill in the grid with your answers and theirs.*

Questions	Mes réponses	Les réponses de mon/ma camarade de classe
Comment tu t'appelles ?		
Tu habites où ?		
Tu as quel âge ?		
Ça va ?		

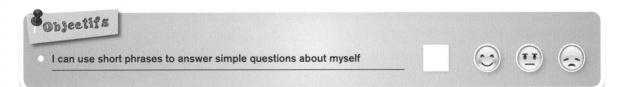

 Objectifs

- I can use short phrases to answer simple questions about myself _____

 ## Astuces

In Ex. 1.11 it is important to pronounce words in the questions and answers correctly. Underline the words you are unsure of and check with your partner. If you are both struggling with pronunciation, ask your teacher.

- Record Ex. 1.11 so that you can practise at home. You could use apps such as Google Classroom or Edmodo.

- Use the Tellagami app to create and share a short animated video : **www.tellagami.com**.

 Interévaluation _Peer assessment._

First, fill in the grid below for yourself, then work with a partner to provide each other with feedback on your performances in Ex. 1.11.

Words I knew really well	
Words I didn't know	
Words I need to pronounce better	
Words I pronounced really well	
My intonation	

 Use the Duolingo app and website: **www.duolingo.com**. duolingo

Discutez en classe. *Have a class discussion.*

- When pronouncing words in French, are there any letters you need to pay special attention to?

- What do you notice about how the verb endings are pronounced? *appelle/appelles*

Ex. 1.12 Des jeunes se présentent

Des jeunes se présentent. *Young people introduce themselves.*

Écoutez les jeunes et cochez les questions qu'ils posent. Ensuite, notez les réponses. *Some young people introduce themselves. Listen and tick the questions they ask in the grid. Then, in the right-hand column, write one of the answers they give.*

	Ça va ?	Tu habites où ?	Comment tu t'appelles ?	Réponses
Marie et Laure				Laure : Ça va mal/ Marie : J'habite à Marseille.
Zoé et Jérôme				
Stéphane et Jules				
Benjamin et David				

 Ex. 1.13 Mots cachés

Traduisez les expressions en anglais puis retrouvez-les dans les mots cachés. *Translate the phrases into English. Then find the French words in the word search.*

AU REVOIR		ÇA VA		MERCI	
BISOUS		ET TOI		SALUT	
BONJOUR		JE M'APPELLE		VOICI	

M	J	Q	D	M	U	W	D	T	X	X	D	O	E	F
A	W	T	E	T	U	L	A	S	E	H	V	S	N	C
D	U	R	Q	F	X	M	W	L	I	X	S	I	Q	X
G	C	R	Z	V	X	P	L	W	O	N	W	W	X	D
I	F	O	B	Z	S	E	K	O	T	M	W	Z	N	O
A	Q	X	U	O	P	I	C	O	T	V	M	Z	D	S
I	F	E	Y	P	N	B	B	A	E	I	D	J	O	O
E	A	L	A	N	N	J	O	J	L	G	G	W	N	O
E	Z	M	T	C	B	S	O	U	D	Z	K	F	U	N
P	E	I	Q	T	I	X	P	U	G	T	P	R	X	O
J	G	B	X	Z	S	I	S	O	R	E	E	I	J	B
W	K	W	L	G	O	Y	C	O	A	A	L	A	Y	A
N	H	N	P	L	U	C	M	I	S	L	M	M	V	P
F	X	I	Y	S	S	Z	M	K	O	U	Y	A	S	U
A	U	R	E	V	O	I	R	S	E	V	Ç	Y	J	N

Prononciation

The letter c in French has a *cédille* (cedilla) when used before *a*, *o* and *u*. This tells us that the c must be pronounced with an s sound, as in the word *français*.

  ### Ex. 1.14 Tu as quel âge ?

 ## Astuces

If we want to answer this question, we need to know our numbers.

The pronunciation of numbers is tricky, so you need to practise.

Écoutez le CD et entrainez-vous à bien prononcer le vocabulaire. *Listen to the CD and repeat the vocabulary to improve your pronunciation.*

 Les nombres de 1 à 15

1	= un		6	=	six	11	= onze
2	= deux		7	=	sept	12	= douze
3	= trois		8	=	huit	13	= treize
4	= quatre		9	=	neuf	14	= quatorze
5	= cinq		10	=	dix	15	= quinze

 ### Ex. 1.15 Les nombres

Additionnez les dés et écrivez le total en français. *Add the dice and write the correct number in French.*

 1. _____

 4. _____

2. _____

5. _____

3. _____

 6. _____

7. _____

9. _____

8. _____

10. _____

  Ex. 1.16 Un poème

Écoutez le CD. Entrainez-vous à la prononciation : lisez ce poème à voix haute. *Listen to the CD. Read the poem out loud to practise your pronunciation.*

> Un deux trois,
> il était une fois.
>
> Quatre, cinq, six,
> une petite saucisse.
>
> Sept, huit, neuf,
> qui aimait un oeuf.
>
> Dix, onze, douze,
> elle était jalouse.
>
> Treize, quatorze, quinze,
> de l'omelette du prince !

 Les adjectifs de nationalité

As we saw earlier, adjectives of nationality change their spelling and the way they are pronounced, depending on whether the person they are describing is male or female. In the English language 'I am Irish' is used for males and females. In French, there are two different versions of the adjective. Usually, the feminine version simply adds the letter *e* to the end of the word. But the masculine/feminine adjectives can work in other ways too – can you see any examples in Ex. 1.17? How do these adjectives change?

Ex. 1.17 Les nationalités

- **(a) Écoutez le CD et entrainez-vous à bien prononcer le vocabulaire.** *Listen to the CD and repeat the vocabulary to improve your pronunciation.*

 Les nationalités

 Je suis irlandais/Je suis irlandaise.   Je suis chinois/chinoise.

 Je suis français/Je suis française.   Je suis écossais/Je suis écossaise.

 Je suis polonais/Je suis polonaise.   Je suis allemand/Je suis allemande.

 Je suis canadien/Je suis canadienne.   Je suis anglais/Je suis anglaise.

- **(b) Vous êtes de quelle nationalité ? Attention ! Choisissez la bonne terminaison.** *What nationality are you? Remember: use the correct ending!*

 Ex. 1.18 Les nationalités

Quelle est leur nationalité ? *Write the nationality for each of these people.*

1. _____

4. _____

2. _____

5. _____

3. _____

6. _____

Ex. 1.19 Les nationalités

Reliez chaque photo à la description qui correspond, puis complétez. *Match each image with the correct description. Fill in the blanks.*

1.

(a) Je suis irlandais. Je m'appelle

_____ . Je suis musicien.

2.

(b) Je suis canadien. Je m'appelle

_____ . Je suis chanteur.

3.

(c) Je suis espagnol. Je m'appelle

_____ . Je suis footballeur.

4.

(d) Je suis française. Je m'appelle

_____ . Je suis actrice.

5.

(e) Je suis écossaise. Je m'appelle

_____ . Je suis politicienne.

Mon Portfolio 1.2 : Je me présente

Faites cet exercice dans votre portfolio. *Do this exercise in your portfolio.*

 Objectifs

- I can introduce myself in French and give my name, my age and my nationality _____

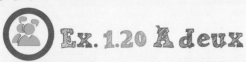 **Ex. 1.20 À deux**

Interviewez un(e) camarade. Utilisez la section « Je me présente » de votre portfolio pour vous aider. *Interview your classmate with the following questions; you can use your portfolio piece « **Je me présente** ». Present your interview to the class or record it.*

	Mes réponses	Les réponses de mon/ma camarade de classe
Tu t'appelles comment ?		
Tu habites où ?		
Tu as quel âge ?		
Tu es de quelle nationalité ?		
Tu parles quelle langue ?		

Interévaluation *Peer assessment.*

First, fill in the grid below for yourself, then work with a partner to provide each other with feedback on your performances in Ex. 1.20.

Words I knew really well	
Words I didn't know	
Words I need to pronounce better	
Words I pronounced really well	
My intonation	

Ex. 1.21 Les gestes

French people tend to use many gestures when they are speaking. Here are some examples.

Mon œil !
I don't believe you!

Je m'ennuie.
I'm bored.

Zéro.
Nothing/zilch.

Comme-ci comme-ça.
So-so/more or less.

Motus et bouche cousue.
My lips are sealed/
Mum's the word.

J'ai du nez.
I know the score.

On s'appelle ?
Chat later?

Super !
Great!

C'est pas moi ! *Nothing to*
do with me!

 Search for 'Comme une française: 12 most common French gestures' to see these gestures in action!

 # Ex. 1.22 Les gestes

Faites les gestes et vos camarades donnent l'expression qui correspond. *Do these gestures with your classmates.*

One student does the gesture, the other students respond with the phrase. Are there any similarities between these French gestures and the gestures used in any other languages that are spoken in your class?

Les noms. *Nouns.*

A noun is the name of a person, place or thing. We use nouns in most sentences. In French, nouns are either masculine or feminine. While there are no definite rules for remembering the gender of nouns, there are a few guidelines that can help:

- Nouns that end in a consonant are usually masculine (except some words ending in *–tion, –sion and –son*)

- Nouns that end in *e* are usually feminine (except some words ending in *–ème, –ège and –age*)

Exemples:	Exemples:
le crayon (m.)	**la** trousse (f.)
le surligneur (m.)	**Le** problème
	La maison
la règle (f.)	*Remember:* *These guidelines do not always apply!*

Objectifs

- **I know that French nouns are either masculine or feminine and I understand general rules about their endings**

L'article défini : le, la, l', les. *The definite article: the.*

When we want to use the word *the* in French, we must ensure we choose the correct definite article. There are four words for *the: le, la, l', les*. This helps us to recognise the gender of each noun. As well as being masculine or feminine, nouns can also be singular or plural.

singular **masculine**	**le**	le garçon (the boy)
singular **feminine**	**la**	la fille (the girl)
singular noun (masculine or feminine), starts with a **vowel or silent h**	**l'**	If a noun starts with a vowel or silent h, then the same form is used for both masculine and feminine. l'amie (the friend, feminine) l'hôtel (the hotel, masculine)
plural (masculine or feminine)	**les**	les garçons (the boys, masculine) les filles (the girls, feminine)

www.wordreference.com is an online dictionary. You can check the meaning of a word and whether it is masculine or feminine. There is also an audio feature that allows you to hear the word in French, so that you can practise your pronunciation.

Objectifs

- I can use the correct article *défini* to accompany a noun

  Ex. 1.23 Vocabulaire

Écoutez le CD et entrainez-vous à bien prononcer le vocabulaire. *Listen to the CD and repeat the vocabulary to improve your pronunciation.*

- l'iPad
- le portable
- les baskets
- la télé
- l'âge
- le livre

- le prof
- le foot
- le ballon
- le chocolat
- les stylos
- les jeux vidéos

- le chien
- le chat
- la chaise
- l'hôtel
- la famille

 Ex. 1.24 Les noms

Fermez le livre et réécoutez le CD. Pour un nom masculin, levez la main, pour un nom fémin[...]ur un nom pluriel, frappez des mains. *Close your book and listen to the CD again. For masculine [...] or feminine nouns stand up, and for plural nouns clap your hands.*

Go to **www.quizlet.com** to create your own French vocabulary [...] nouns in the box below. Check the gender and remember [...] on each flashcard.

- stylo
- élève
- agenda
- chat
- trousse

- portable
- chocolat
- foo[...]

Unité 1 : Je me présente

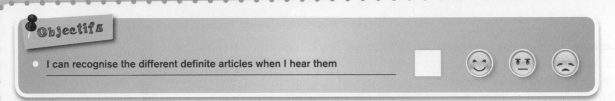

Objectifs

- I can recognise the different definite articles when I hear them

Ex. 1.25 Vocabulaire

Écoutez le CD et entrainez-vous à bien prononcer le vocabulaire. *Listen to the CD and repeat the vocabulary to improve your pronunciation.*

À mon avis ...
- J'aime ✓
- J'adore ✓ ✓
- Je n'aime pas ✗
- Je déteste ✗ ✗
- Oui, moi aussi.

- Je suis d'accord.
- Tu as tort.
- Tu as raison.
- Tu rigoles.
- Tu es fou !

- Tu es folle !
- C'est cool.
- C'est super cool !
- Moi, mon truc, c'est ...
- Ce n'est pas mon truc.

Ex. 1.26 À mon avis ...

Utilisez les mots clés pour donner votre avis. *Use your new vocabulary to give your opinion.*

1. J'aime Kanye West _____

5. _____

2. _____

6. _____

_____

7. _____

 Ex. 1.27 Écoutez

Écoutez le CD et complétez la grille. *Listen to the CD and write your answers in the table below.*

	J'aime	Je n'aime pas	J'adore	Je déteste	Other information
Stéphanie					lives in Lyon
Chloé					
José					

Objectifs

- I can give my opinion in French
- I can understand when people are giving their opinion in French

 Ex. 1.28 Group Talk

You are about to see a video of Irish students just like you using Group Talk vocabulary to give their opinions. These students have the exact same *mots-clés* as you. Do you see how authentic their conversations are? With the *mots-clés* you have already learned, you can have a real conversation in French! As we move through the book, we will add to the *mots-clés* so that you can build on your conversations.

In this video clip, the students have a sheet with pictures of things they can give their opinion on. They are able to agree or disagree with each other using short and simple sentences.

Regardez les élèves irlandais, Sean, Emily et Josh, donner leur avis. Répondez aux questions. *Watch the video of the Irish students giving their opinions and answer the questions.*

C'est cool.

1. What does Josh like?
2. Does Emily agree with Josh?
3. Who likes The X Factor?
4. Who thinks The X Factor is terrible?
5. What do Josh and Sean agree on?
6. What do they all agree on?

7. What is the French for the following phrases?

    (a) You are crazy!

    (b) You're joking!

    (c) It's not my thing.

    (d) I hate

    (e) I like

    (f) You are wrong!

    (g) It's cool.

 There are two words for crazy in this piece: *fou* and *folle*. Why is this? Discuss this with your class and see if you can figure out which one to use in which situation.

Ex. 1.29 Group Talk

 Votre discussion de groupe. *Your Group Talk.*
Group Talk Step 1

You are going to prepare to do your own Group Talk with your classmates. The video of the students in Ex. 1.28 showed them using the Group Talk phrases below. They had a sheet

with pictures of things to give their opinion on. They could agree or disagree with each other. You are going to use the images below for your Group Talk, so you need to ensure that you know what they are in French! You must decide which you like, dislike, love or hate!

J'aime ☐
J'adore ☐
Je n'aime pas ☐
Je déteste ☐

J'aime ☐
J'adore ☐
Je n'aime pas ☐
Je déteste ☐

J'aime ☐
J'adore ☐
Je n'aime pas ☐
Je déteste ☐

J'aime ☐
J'adore ☐
Je n'aime pas ☐
Je déteste ☐

J'aime ☐
J'adore ☐
Je n'aime pas ☐
Je déteste ☐

Group Talk Step 2

Lisez votre liste à voix haute à un(e) camarade. *Read your list out loud with your partner to practise your pronunciation.*

Group Talk Step 3

Now you're ready to do your own Group Talk. You can do this either in pairs or in small groups like those you saw in the Group Talk video. You have already looked at the images and you have already decided which you like, love, dislike or hate.

- Remember to use the images and the Group Talk phrases to give your opinion like Sean, Emily and Josh.

- The first person starts by giving their opinion on one of the images. Moving around the table, each student can either agree or disagree. When you get more confident, you can jump into the conversation at any point and disagree or agree with the other students in the group! It's often fun to have one student who is secretly chosen to always disagree. They can cause a lot of drama during the Group Talk! Use the *mots-clés* from page 20 for your Group Talk phrases.

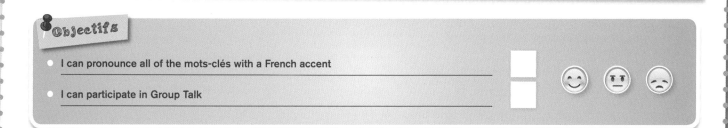

Objectifs

- I can pronounce all of the mots-clés with a French accent

- I can participate in Group Talk

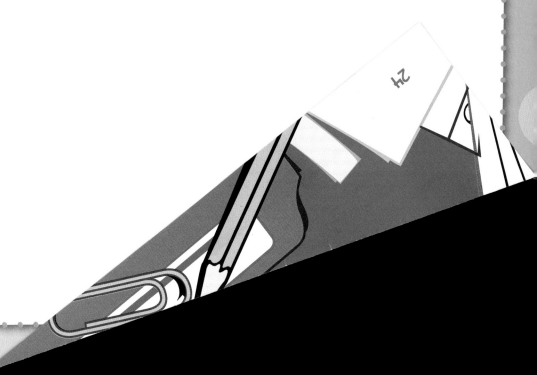

Récapitulatif

Mots-clés pour Unité 1

Je me présente

- Bonjour
- Salut
- Coucou
- Au revoir
- Ça va ?
- Ça va bien, merci.

- Non, ça ne va pas très bien.
- Comme-ci comme-ça.
- Et toi ?
- Moi aussi, ça va ! / Moi non plus, ça ne va pas.
- Comment tu t'appelles?
- Je m'appelle …

- Tu habites où ?
- J'habite à Dublin.
- Tu as quel âge ?
- J'ai douze/ treize ans.
- Je suis irlandais/irlandaise, indien/indienne, britannique, etc.

Les nombres de 1 à 15

1	= un	6	= six	11	= onze
2	= deux	7	= sept	12	= douze
3	= trois	8	= huit	13	= treize
4	= quatre	9	= neuf	14	= quatorze
5	= cinq	10	= dix	15	= quinze

Les nationalités

- Je suis irlandais/Je suis irlandaise.
- Je suis français/Je suis française.
- Je suis écossais/Je suis écossaise.
- Je suis polonais/Je suis polonaise.

- Je suis allemand/Je suis allemande.
- Je suis canadien/Je suis canadienne.
- Je suis anglais/Je suis anglaise.
- Je suis chinois/Je suis chinoise.

À mon avis …

- J'aime
- J'adore
- Je n'aime pas
- Je déteste
- Oui, moi aussi.

- Je suis d'accord.
- Tu as tort.
- Tu as raison.
- Tu rigoles.
- Tu es fou !

- Tu es folle !
- C'est cool.
- C'est super cool !
- Moi, mon truc, c'est …
- Ce n'est pas mon truc.

Bilan de l'Unité 1. *Checklist for Unit 1.*

Pour chaque objectif, choisissez votre émoticône.	😊	😐	😞
Listening			
I can understand someone introducing themselves in French			
I can understand simple questions about my name, age, personality and nationality			
I can understand the numbers 1 to 15			
I can understand when people are giving their opinion in French			
Reading			
I can read a short dialogue of people introducing themselves			
I can read the names of everyday objects			
Spoken production			
I can introduce someone			
I can say my name and age			
I can say my nationality			
I can count from 1 to 15			
I can name some everyday objects, using the correct definite article			
I can give my opinion (likes and dislikes)			
Spoken interaction			
I can ask someone their name and age			
I can ask someone where they live and what nationality they are			
I can give my opinion in a group			
I can use gestures when I speak			

Unité 1 : Je me présente

Writing			
I can write a short description of myself, giving my name, address, age and nationality			
I can fill out a form with my name, age, address and nationality			
I can write numbers 1 to 15 in French			

Discutez en classe. *Have a class discussion.*

- Look back over your Portfolio exercises. In which areas did you give yourself stars?

- Look at your wishes. Have any of these improved?

- What was your favourite part of Unité 1? Why?

- What did you least enjoy in Unité 1? Why?

- You completed many different kinds of activities in Unité 1. What kinds of activities were the best for helping you to learn? Why?

- Think about the next unit you will work on. What are you looking forward to learning more about? Why?

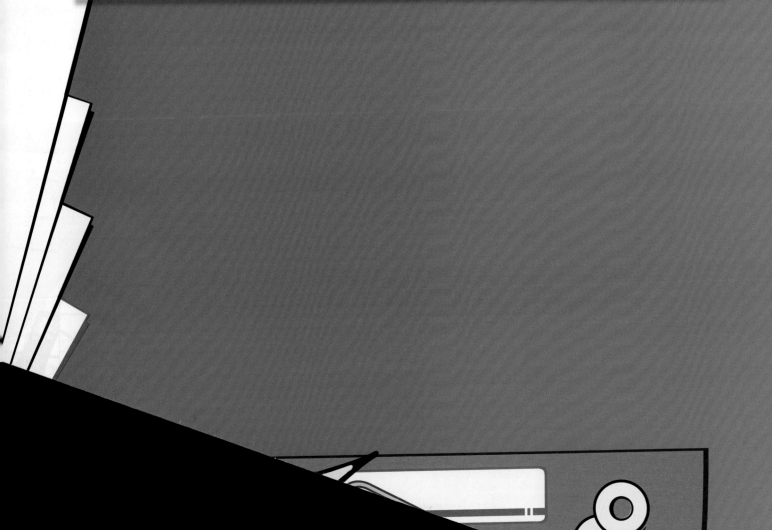

UNITÉ 2

Au collège

La rentrée
c'est
maintenant

vive la rentrée

By the end of this unit you will

- Understand *la rentrée* and make a *Bonne rentrée* card
- Understand and use classroom phrases
- Name your school items and spell them in French
- Use the phrases *c'est* and *ce sont*
- Use the verb *être*
- Use sentences in the negative in French
- Do a role play in class using your classroom vocabulary
- Name the days of the week

Ex. 2.1 Bonne rentrée !

Regardez et écoutez la vidéo de la rentrée en France, puis répondez aux questions dans votre cahier. *Watch the video of la rentrée in France, and answer the questions in your copybook.*

1. What does *la rentrée* mean?
2. What months are traditionally the holiday months in France?
3. Note two differences between schools in France and schools in Ireland.
4. Do students wear uniforms in France?
5. What is the name for the equivalent of 1st Year to 3rd Year in France?
6. What is the name of the French equivalent of the Junior Certificate exam?

Objectifs

- I can explain *la rentrée* in France _____

  ## Ex. 2.2

Écoutez le CD et entrainez-vous à bien prononcer le vocabulaire. *Listen to the CD and repeat the vocabulary to improve your pronunciation.*

 Bonne rentrée card

Greetings	Message	Signing off
Cher (m)	Bonne rentrée !	Amitiés
Chère (f)	Amuse-toi bien !	Ton ami
Salut	Bon courage pour la rentrée au collège !	Ton amie
Bonjour		À bientôt
Coucou		Bisous

Prononciation

Most English words that end in *–ion* (e.g. salutation) are the same in French – only you say them with a French accent! The *–ion* sound is softer in French than in English.

 Make a list of five more English words that end with *–ion* and, using your dictionary, check their French translations. As a class, see how many of them are the same in both languages, and practise their French pronunciation.

 **Ex. 2.3**

Reliez chaque mot français avec la bonne traduction. *Match each French word with its correct English translation.*

Salut !	Hello/Hi there!
Bon courage pour la rentrée au collège	Best wishes
Coucou !	See you soon!
Cher	Have fun!
À bientôt !	Lots of love
Chère	Your friend (m)
Bonne rentrée !	Your friend (f)
Bisous	Best of luck starting secondary school
Amuse-toi bien !	Have a good return to school!
Amitiés	Dear (m)
Ton ami	Hey!
Ton amie	Dear (f)

 Search for *bonne rentrée* ecards on **www.merci-facteur.com** to get some ideas for your next *Mon portfolio* exercise.

 **Mon portfolio 2.1 :** Ma carte de « Bonne rentrée »

Faites cet exercice dans votre portfolio. *Do this exercise in your portfolio.*

  Ex. 2.4 Le collège en France

Regardez et écoutez la vidéo, puis répondez aux questions dans votre cahier. *Watch the video and answer the questions in your copybook.*

1. What is the Irish equivalent of *collège*?

2. What is the Irish equivalent of *sixième*?

3. How long do French students spend in secondary school altogether?

4. What must you do to move on to the next school year in France?

5. When French students have finished *collège*, what school do they go to?

6. How many years do students spend in *collège*?

Les Choristes is a great French film about boys in a boarding school in 1940s France who join a choir and learn to sing. Watch the film, then search online for 'Irish Film Institute study guide to *Les Choristes*' to learn more about it.

Astuces

When you are learning a new language, the more you hear it used in everyday phrases, and the more you can respond to those phrases, the better you will become! Classroom phrases are easy to use, and they are important to know because we use them so often. Phrases that we use a lot are called *high-frequency phrases*, and it makes sense to know them well because we use them regularly.

As you work through Unité 2, remember these tips:

- Learn the *mots-clés*, which are high-frequency phrases.

- If there is a phrase that your class uses regularly but it is not listed in Unité 2, ask your teacher to write and pronounce the phrase, write it in the *mots-clés* section, and use it.

- Try to use French instructions whenever you can in class. See who can avoid using English for as long as possible in class, including your teacher!

- Remember to use gestures and body language to help get your message across.

- Don't worry about making mistakes: these are simply *learning opportunities* and they are very much part of the language-learning journey.

French Bear: Une baguette ?
Irish Bear: Oui, merci

French Bear: C'est tout monsieur ?
Irish Bear: Oui, merci.

French Bear: Vous parlez très bien français.
Irish Bear: Go raibh maith agat!

Astuces

Ex. 2.5 lists some of the most used phrases in the classroom. Practise their pronunciation and add a gesture or action to each one so that you can remember it more clearly.

Ex. 2.5 Dans la salle de classe

Écoutez le CD et entrainez-vous à bien prononcer le vocabulaire. *Listen to the CD and repeat the vocabulary to improve your pronunciation.*

 Mots-clés

Dans la salle de classe Le professeur

Ouvrez vos livres		Écoutez	
Fermez vos livres		Répétez	
Regardez		Travaillez avec votre camarade de classe	
Écrivez		Je vais faire l'appel	

Dans la salle de classe Les élèves

 Je peux aller aux toilettes, s'il vous plait ?

 Qu'est-ce que ça veut dire ?

Prononciation

In French, to help our words flow more smoothly we use what is called a *liaison* – a link. As you know, the ends of words are usually silent. However, when you have a word ending in a consonant and the next word begins with a vowel, then you use a *liaison*. For example: *Elle est absente*. Normally you would not pronounce the *t* in *est*, but because *absente* begins with a vowel, you do pronounce the *t* to make the sentence flow better.

  Ex. 2.6
CD 1
T 15

Décrivez les images et remplissez les blancs dans les phrases. *Describe the pictures and fill in the blanks in the sentences.*

Puis, écoutez le CD et entrainez-vous à bien prononcer le vocabulaire. *Then listen to the CD and repeat the vocabulary to improve your pronunciation.*

1. Elle est ___absente___.

2. Je vais _____ l'appel.

3. _____ vos livres.

4. Je peux aller _____ toilettes, s'il vous plait ?

5. _____ avec votre camarade de classe.

6. _____

7. _____ ça veut dire ?

8. É_____ .

9. É_____ .

10. R_____ .

 # Ex. 2.7 Jacques a dit...

Work with your class to decide on an action for each of the phrases in Ex. 2.5. Your teacher says 'Jacques a dit …' and gives an instruction , as in a game of Simon Says. The person who comes last in following the instruction with the gesture is out. How long can you stay in the game?

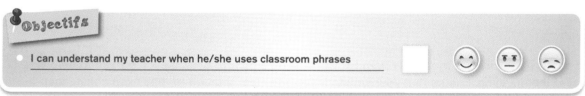

Objectifs

● I can understand my teacher when he/she uses classroom phrases _____ 😊 😐 ☹

Prononciation

As you learn French, you will see that there are common sounds and tips for pronunciation

● Often, the last consonants of words are not pronounced. For example: *regardez*, *écoutez*, etc. In these words, you do not hear the *z* sound.

● Each syllable gets the same stress. When you say long words, break them up into even beats and sections. For example: there are three even beats in *camarade* and *travaillez*.

● The letter *r* has a throaty sound in French: it is very different from the *r* sound in English. For example: *fermez les livres*, *présente*, *regardez*, etc.

Ex. 2.8

Écoutez le CD et numérotez les images. *Listen to the CD and number the images as you hear them.*

Objectifs

- I can use at least three classroom phrases during French class _____

Ex. 2.9.

Make classroom posters showing the *mots-clés* from Ex. 2.5. Include a picture beside each phrase to help you learn and remember the meaning. Ensure that your writing is big and clear enough to read from a distance!

Create a class blog. You can use apps such as Google Classroom or Edmodo to upload audio, video, documents and PowerPoints.

parlez-vous français?

Les verbes et les pronoms sujets. *Verbs and subject pronouns.*

Verbs are a key part of every sentence in every language. A verb is an action word.

| I walk | I see | I read | I am |

When we use a verb, we mostly use either a noun or a pronoun to show who carries out the action.

| **I** am happy (I = pronoun) |
| **Chloe** is happy (Chloe = noun) |
| **The teacher** is happy (teacher = noun) |

In French, verbs have different endings. The subject (noun or pronoun) tells you each time which ending is needed. A subject pronoun is used instead of a noun. Let's look at the subject pronouns in French.

Subject pronoun	
Je	I
Tu	You
Il	He
Elle	She
On	One or Informal we
Nous	We
Vous	You (plural) or You (formal)
Ils	They (masculine) or They (masculine and feminine)
Elles	They (feminine)

Ex. 2.10 Les verbes et les pronoms sujets

With your partner, read back over the explanation of the subject pronouns and verbs. *Think about the explanation and take turns in saying each subject pronoun in French and giving each meaning in English.*

- I can understand what a verb is and I can explain it to my partner
- I can understand what a subject pronoun is and I can explain it to my partner

Le pronom *on*. The pronoun *on*.

Although *on* does not mean the same thing as *il* and *elle*, the verb ending that is needed for a verb used with *on* is the same as for *il* and *elle*.

On can translate as *one*, or *people in general*.

En France, on aime les croissants. In France, people love croissants.

On usually translates as *we*. *On* is used very often by French people instead of *nous*. The use of *nous* is usually reserved for more formal situations or when writing.

On regarde le film. We are watching the film.

On + verb can also mean *let's* when you raise your voice at the end of a sentence.

On regarde le film ? Let's watch the film.

 Ex. 2.11 Le pronom on

With your partner, read back over the explanation of the subject pronoun *on*. *Take turns in explaining to each other how it is used in French.*

- I understand the French pronoun *on* and can explain it to my partner

 Ex. 2.12

Écrivez les pronoms sujets français qui correspondent aux pronoms sujets anglais. *Write the correct French subject pronouns beside the correct English subject pronouns.*

	He
	I
	They (m)
	You (informal)
	We

	She
	You (formal or plural)
	They (f)
	You (informal)
	They (m+f)

 Search YouTube for '**Etienne – les pronoms**' for a song to help you learn your subject pronouns.

 Un verbe irrégulier *Être* – *to be*

● *Tu es en quelle classe ?   Je suis en sixième.*

To answer the question *What year are you in?* you will need to use the verb **être**.

The verb *être* means *to be*. It is an irregular verb. This means that it does not follow a pattern and it does not have set endings. *Être* is one of the most important irregular French verbs.

 ## Ex. 2.13 Le verbe être

Traduisez le verbe *être* en anglais. *Translate the remainder of the verb être into English.*

être	to be
Je suis	I am, I am being
Tu es	You are, you are being
Il est	
Elle est	
On est	
Nous sommes	
Vous êtes	
Ils sont	
Elles sont	

Astuces

Most verbs in French are regular: they have a pattern and set endings. However, some of the verbs that we use the most in French are irregular. We have to learn each of these irregular verbs off by heart. As we use them very often, it actually helps us to remember them. Pay attention to any irregular verbs you come across. Learn them one at a time.

  Ex. 2.14

Le verbe *être* – Écoutez le CD et remplissez la grille avec la bonne partie du verbe *être*. *Listen to the CD. Write the correct part of the verb être in the blanks.*

Je _____	Nous _____
_____ es	_____ êtes
Il _____	Ils _____
Elle _____	Elles _____
_____ est	

  Ex. 2.15

Réécoutez le CD et répétez le verbe *être* pour améliorer votre prononciation. *Now listen to the CD again and repeat the verb être to practise your pronunciation.*

Objectifs

- I can understand and explain what the verb *être* means ☐ 😊 😐 ☹️

www.wordreference.com is an online dictionary that has a handy verb conjugator where you can double-check a verb ending.

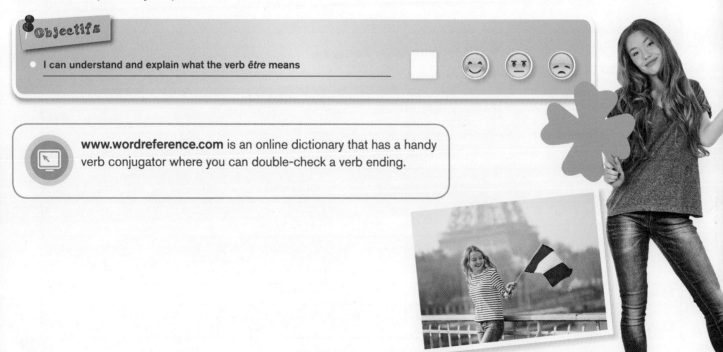

 **Ex. 2.16**

Reliez les pronoms sujets à la bonne forme du verbe *être*. *Match the subject pronouns to the correct part of the verb être.*

Les pronoms sujets	
A. Ils	E. Je
B. Vous	F. Nous
C. Il	G. Tu
D. Elle	H. Elles

Le verbe être	
___ suis	___ êtes
___ sommes	___ sont
___ es	___ est
___ sont	___ est

Objectifs

- I can recognise the correct part of *être* for each subject pronoun
- I know the verb *être* off by heart

😊 😐 ☹️

 **Ex. 2.17 À deux**

À deux : posez les questions à votre camarade et répondez à ses questions. Complétez la grille. *Talk with your classmate. Ask them questions and reply to theirs. Fill in the grid with your answers and theirs.*

Questions	Mes réponses	Les réponses de ma/mon camarade
Comment tu t'appelles ?		
Tu habites où ?		
Tu as quel âge ?		
Ça va ?		

Ex. 2.18 Interévaluation

First, fill in the grid below for yourself, then work with a partner to provide each other with feedback on your performances in Ex. 2.17.

Words I knew really well	
Words I didn't know	
Words I need to pronounce better	
Words I pronounced really well	
My intonation	

L'article indéfini. *The indefinite article.*

This the grammar term for *a* or *an*.

Remember that in French, all nouns are either masculine or feminine. This means that we have a masculine version of the words *a/an* and a feminine version of the words *a/an*.

masculine	un	*un* cahier (*an exercise book*)
feminine	une	*une* trousse (*a pencil case*)
plural	des	*des* stylos (*some pens*)

Astuces

It can be hard to remember the gender of all the new nouns that you meet. While it is best to learn the noun and its gender at the same time, there are a few clues that can help you to guess the gender. Words that end in:

- eur, eau, (i)er, o are usually masculine

- euse, trice, tion, ette are usually feminine.

Écrivez M (masculin), F (féminin), PL (pluriel) dans les boites. Traduisez les mots en anglais. Puis, écoutez le CD et répétez le vocabulaire pour améliorer votre prononciation.

Write M, F, PL in the boxes. Translate the words into English. Then listen to the CD and repeat the vocabulary to improve your pronunciation.

1. Un cahier _____

2. Une trousse _____

3. Un gymnase _____

4. Des salles de classes _____

5. Une bibliothèque _____

6. Une école _____

7. Un collège _____

8. Des livres _____

9. Un professeur _____

10. Des stylos _____

 Ex. 2.20

With your partner, read back over the explanation of *un, une* and *des*. Think about the explanation and take turns in explaining it to each other.

Objectifs

● I can understand and explain l'article indéfini _____ ☐ 😊 😐 😞

Ex. 2.21 Mes affaires d'école

Écoutez le CD et entrainez-vous à bien prononcer le vocabulaire. *Listen to the CD and repeat the vocabulary to improve your pronunciation.*

 Mes affaires d'école

- une trousse
- un stylo
- un crayon
- un feutre
- une clé USB
- une gomme
- une règle

- une calculatrice
- une colle
- une agrafeuse
- des ciseaux
- un taille-crayon
- un classeur
- un agenda

- un cahier
- un livre
- un cartable
- un iPod
- un portable
- un surligneur

Search YouTube for '***Dans ma salle de classe, Matt Maxwell***' for a song to help you learn school vocabulary.

 Qu'est-ce que c'est? C'est … Ce sont …

We form the word *c'est* using the verb **être**.

C'est	*it is* *that is*	C'est mon stylo	*It is my pen* *That is my pen*
Ce sont	*they are*	Ce sont mes stylos	*Those are my pens*

C'est can be followed by a noun, a pronoun or an adjective:

Noun	C'est ma calculatrice	It's my calculator
Pronoun	C'est moi	It's me
Adjective	C'est super	It's super

 ## Ex. 2.22

Complétez les phrases avec *c'est* ou *ce sont*. *Complete the sentences using either c'est or ce sont.*

1. _____ un stylo.

2. _____ des feutres.

3. _____ une agrafeuse.

4. _____ magnifique !

5. _____ des crayons.

6. _____ un surligneur.

7. _____ des livres.

8. _____ une clé USB.

9. _____ fantastique !

10. _____ une calculatrice.

Visit **www.kahoot.com** or **www.studystack.com** to create games for practising your vocabulary. You simply type in the new words that you want to learn and the websites will generate all sorts of games, such as hangman, to help you practise.

Ex. 2.23 Le blog vidéo d'Inès

Regardez le blog vidéo d'Inès. Elle parle de ses affaires d'école. *Watch the video of Inès. She is talking about her school things.*

Traduisez les mots. *Translate the words.*

 CD 1 T 20 **Écoutez le CD et entrainez-vous à bien prononcer le vocabulaire.** *Listen to the CD and repeat the vocabulary to improve your pronunciation.*

Prononciation

Can you remember how to pronounce the following sounds and words in French?

- ou – trousse
- on – crayon
- eur – classeur

En anglais	En français
book	
pen	
stapler	

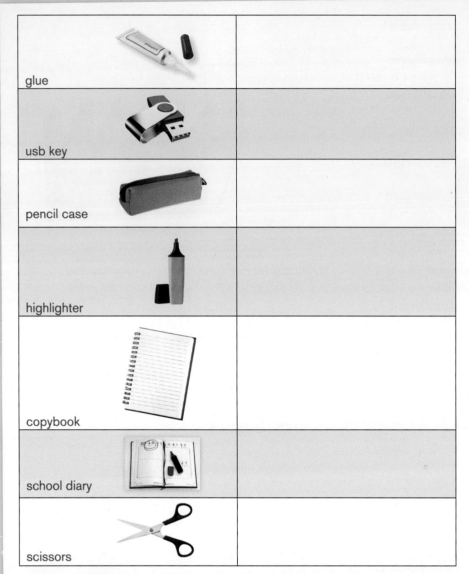

glue		
usb key		
pencil case		
highlighter		
copybook		
school diary		
scissors		

 Ex. 2.24 L'article indéfini – Un, une ou des?

Les jeunes décrivent ce qu'ils ont dans leur cartable. Complétez la bonne colonne. *The teenagers describe what they have in their schoolbags. Write their school items into the correct column.*

	un	une	des
Kévin			
Marie			
Benjamin			

Astuces

When using your dictionary, you will see that nouns have *nm* (meaning *noun masculine*) or *nf* (meaning *noun feminine*) written after them. Some online dictionaries such as **www.wordreference.com** also have a sound feature, so they tell you how to pronounce the word as well.

Ex. 2.25 Trouvez les différences

1. **Trouvez les différences et entourez-les.** *Spot the differences and circle them.*

2. **Faites la liste des affaires d'école qui manquent sur l'image.** *Make a list of the items of school materials that are missing in the second image.*

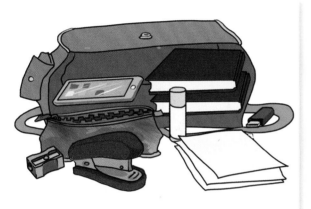 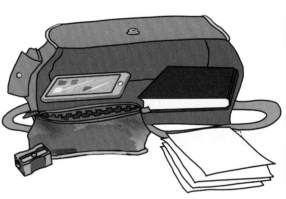

Mon Portfolio 2.2 : Mon cartable

Faites cet exercice dans votre portfolio. *Do this exercise in your portfolio.*

 **Ex. 2.26**

Lisez la liste des fournitures scolaires de l'école des sorciers et répondez aux questions en anglais. *Read the list of school materials and answer the questions in French.*

École de Sorciers, Classe de Madame la Sorcière Invincible. *Rentrée scolaire Liste de fournitures scolaires*

Un agenda scolaire

5 cahiers

1 trousse

5 stylos :

2 noirs, 1 bleu, 1 rouge, 1 vert

2 crayons à papier HB

2 gommes

1 paire de ciseaux

1 agrafeuse

3 colles

1 clé USB

1 règle (en plastique)

15 feutres

20 crayons de couleur

1 surligneur jaune

1 calculatrice

1 pochette en carton

1. Name any four items you must have for Madame la Sorcière Invincible's class.

   _____

   _____

2. How many copybooks should you have?

   _____

3. You must have a school journal and two glue sticks. True or false? _____

4. You must have a pencil case, two USB keys and a stapler. True or false? _____

5. Underline any of the following items that are not on the list.

   (a) mobile   (b) sharpener   (c) schoolbag

   (c) stapler   (d) highlighter

6. How many markers should you have?

   _____

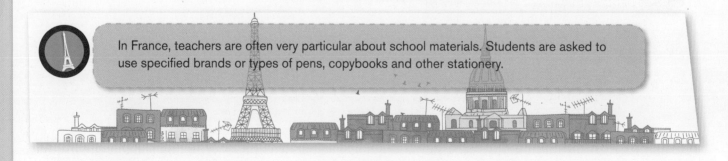

In France, teachers are often very particular about school materials. Students are asked to use specified brands or types of pens, copybooks and other stationery.

 http://www.rentreediscount.com is a French website for school supplies. How does it compare with similar websites from Ireland?

La négation

The words *ne … pas* are used to make sentences negative in French. To put them in the correct place in the sentence, you:

1. Find the verb in the sentence.

2. Put *ne* before the verb.

3. Put *pas* after the verb.

Exemple : Ils sont français ? Non, ils ne sont pas français.

If the verb you are using begins with a vowel (*a, e, i, o, u*) or *h*, then *ne* changes to *n'* but the *pas* remains the same. The apostrophe replaces the missing *e* of *ne*. We do this only when the word after *ne* begins with a vowel or *h*.

Exemple: Il est grand ? Non, il n'est pas grand.

We do the same when using *je* in front of a vowel.

Exemple : J'aime le film. *Je* n'aime pas le film.

The *e* of *je* is replaced with an apostrophe, so that *je* simply becomes *j'*.

Remember, this is only necessary when the word after *je* begins with a vowel or *h*. And when you add in *ne … pas*, you don't need to change the *je* as it is no longer followed by a vowel or h.

Exemple :

J'aime le gâteau. (*Je* becomes *j'*)   Je n'aime pas le gâteau. (*ne* becomes *n'*.)

Objectifs

• I can use the negative _____ ☐ 😊 😐 ☹

Ex. 2.27 Les phrases négatives

Faites des phrases négatives. *Write the sentences in the negative.*

Astuces

Remember these steps to make sentences negative:

● Underline each verb in the sentence before you begin. Then use the *ne … pas* formula to make each sentence negative.

● Use *n'* before a verb that begins with a vowel or *h*.

● Remember to change *j'* back to *je*.

● Remember to change *c'* back to *ce*.

1. Il _____ habite _____ à Dublin.

2. Elle _____ est _____ grande.

3. Vous _____ êtes _____ petite.

4. J'_____ aime _____ le film.

5. Amélie _____ aime _____ la musique.

6. C'_____est _____ un stylo.

7. Ce _____ sont _____ des crayons.

8. J' _____ aime _____ *The X Factor.*

Astuces

When we want to make a noun plural in French we usually add *s* for regular nouns. Look back to Ex. 2.27 and see where the nouns are plural and how they are spelled in the plural. Later we will look at how irregular nouns change.

  # Ex. 2.28 Vocabulaire

Écoutez le CD et entrainez-vous à bien prononcer le vocabulaire. *Listen to the CD and repeat the vocabulary to improve your pronunciation.*

 Parlons en classe

- Je peux emprunter …
- Oui, bien sur
- Tiens
- Merci

- De rien
- Non, désolé(e), je n'ai pas de …
- Ce n'est pas grave

 **Ex. 2.29**

Lisez la conversation et répondez aux questions. *Read the conversation and answer the questions.*

> **Amélie :** Je peux emprunter un stylo, s'il te plait ?
> **Lionel :** Oui, tiens, un stylo.
>
> **Lionel :** Tu as une feuille de papier, s'il te plait ?
> **Amélie :** Non, désolée, je n'ai pas une feuille de papier.

1. What did Amélie borrow ?

2. What did Lionel ask to borrow?

3. Did Amélie have one?

> **Laura :** Je peux emprunter une gomme, s'il te plait ?
> **Julien :** Oui, tiens, une gomme.
>
> **Laura :** Merci.
> **Julien :** De rien.

1. What did Laura borrow?

2. How did Julien say *You're welcome*?

> **Nicolas :** Maxime, je peux emprunter une calculatrice, s'il te plait ?
> **Maxime :** Bien sur, Nicolas, tiens.
> **Nicolas :** Merci, Maxime.
>
> **Maxime :** De rien, Nicolas. Je peux emprunter un stylo ?
> **Nicolas :** Désolé, Maxime, je n'ai pas de stylo.
> **Maxime :** Ce n'est pas grave, merci.
> **Nicolas :** De rien.

1. What did Nicolas borrow?

2. How did Maxime say *of course*?

 Ex. 2.30 Jeu de rôle en classe

Carry out a role play with your partner, asking to borrow the following items. Record your role play as a sample of your work. You can do this simply by opening a folder, calling it *My digital portfolio* and storing all your recordings there. You could also use the Tellagami app.

 1.

3.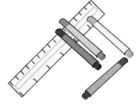

2.

4.

Astuces

Role plays can be a little daunting at first, but here are a few strategies to help you.

- Plan what you want to say. This means revising your vocabulary and even writing out your script word for word before the role play.

- Make vocabulary flash cards using websites such as **www.quizlet.com.**

- Record sample role plays and put them on a platform such as Google Classroom, where they are easily accessible.

- Practise your vocabulary with your partner. Then practise the full conversation with your partner. Give your partner the vocabulary flashcards so that they can prompt you if you get stuck.

- After a while, you won't need to rely on any of these tips!

Ex. 2.31 La Vie en France

Voici la liste-modèle des fournitures scolaires du Ministre de l'éducation en France. Lisez-la et répondez aux questions. *Here is a recommended list of school items published by the French Minister for Education. The French government creates lists such as these to help keep costs down for parents and to reduce the weight of schoolbags.*

1. Name three recommended items from the list.
2. How many coloured pencils should students have?
3. What type of ruler is recommended?
4. You should have a metal pencil sharpener. True or false?
5. What should students use to cover their books?
6. Translate these items into French.

Hardback folder _____

Large copybook _____

Plastic pockets _____

Small copybook _____

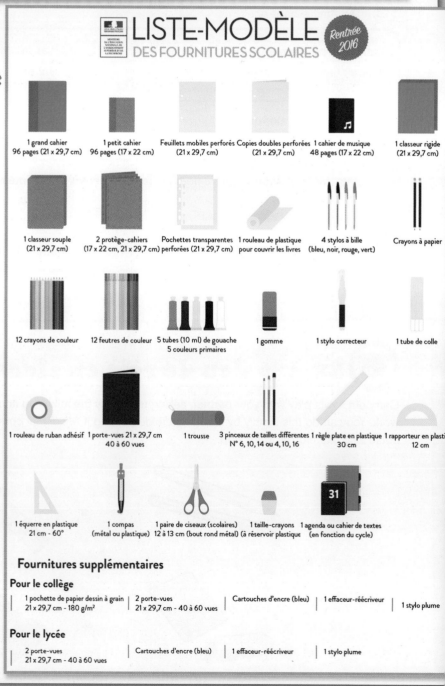

Ex. 2.32 L'alphabet en français

Écoutez le CD et répétez l'alphabet pour améliorer votre prononciation. *Listen and repeat the letters of the French alphabet to practise your pronunciation.*

The alphabet in French is pronounced differently from the alphabet in English, even though we have the same letters.

 L'alphabet en français

a	= ah	h	= ash	o	= oh		
b	= bay	i	= ee	p	= pay		
c	= say	j	= jhee	q	= koo		
d	= day	k	= kah	r	= air	v	= vay
e	= eh	l	= el	s	= ess	w	= doo-bluh-vay
f	= eff	m	= em	t	= tay	x	= eex
g	= jhay	n	= en	u	= ooh	y	= ee-grek
						z	= zed

 Les accents

  J'adore ton accent

Accents	Letters	Examples
Accent aigu	é	The accent aigu only goes over the letter e in French and changes the sound e = [uh] into é = [ey] as in the words fiancé or café. Note: You do not need to open your mouth as wide for the sound é as you need to for the sound è or ê.
Accent grave	è à ù	The accent grave does not affect the sound of a or u, but placed over the letter e, it changes the sound e = [uh] into è = [eh] as in the English word set. Note: ù is only used in the word où (= where) to distinguish it from ou (= or).
Circonflexe	â ê ô	The accent circonflexe over the letter e changes the sound e = [uh] into ê = [eh], in the same way that the accent grave does. Over the letter a it changes the sound a as in the English word hat to the sound â as in the English word part. Note: In some cases, the circumflex has replaced the letter s which was lost from the original Latin word (forêt, hôpital, etc.)
Tréma	ï ë	The tréma accent indicates that when two vowels are next to each other in a word, they must both be pronounced separately like they are in the words Noël or naïve.
Cédille	ç	The cedilla is used only with the letter c in front of the vowels a, o, and u and it tells us that the c must be pronounced with an 's' sound as opposed to a 'k' sound.

As you can see there are a few different accents used in French. It is important to keep an eye out for accents on new words, so that you can learn the accent as part of the spelling of your new words. When you were learning Irish you learned about the *fada*. What accents do other language-speakers in your class use in their languages?

 Ex. 2.33 Les accents

Nommez les lettres avec leur accent. *Name the following letters with their accents. Then write them in the table.*

î	The letter i circumflex	ù	
é		ç	
ô		è	
ë		â	

 Ex. 2.34

Épelez les mots suivants à voix haute avec votre camarade de classe. *Spell the following words out loud to your partner in French.*

- une agrafeuse
- une trousse
- un agenda
- une clé USB

  Ex. 2.35 Les jours de la semaine

Écoutez le CD et entrainez-vous à bien prononcer le vocabulaire.
Listen to the CD and repeat the vocabulary to improve your pronunciation.

mars

lundi	mardi	mercredi	jeudi	vendredi	samedi	dimanche
		1	2	3	4	5
6	7	8	9	10	11	12
13	14	15	16	17	18	19
20	21	22	23	24	25	26
27	28	29	30	31		

 On est quel jour aujourd'hui ? Aujourd'hui, on est …

- lundi
- mardi
- mercredi
- jeudi
- vendredi
- samedi
- dimanche

Astuces

- In French, we don't use capital letters for days of the week or months of the year.

- When we want to say *on Monday* in French, the little preposition *on* is taken for granted in the word itself. *On Monday* in French is simply *lundi*.

Ex. 2.36 Mots cachés

Traduisez les jours de la semaine et cherchez-les dans les mots cachés. *Translate the days of the week and find them in the word search*

Anglais	Français
Monday	_____
Tuesday	_____
Wednesday	_____

Thursday _____

Friday _____

Saturday _____

Sunday _____

I	I	L	P	U	Y	I	Y	H	E	X	U	V	I	T
D	D	L	Q	I	L	P	A	T	O	F	E	L	W	H
Y	V	E	L	S	P	K	I	N	D	N	F	Y	S	P
W	A	M	M	N	P	M	I	N	D	L	T	K	A	W
A	I	L	K	A	D	V	M	R	V	N	C	R	G	G
C	I	U	R	D	S	K	E	E	A	X	Z	X	I	M
X	N	U	U	M	L	D	J	E	U	D	I	X	Y	G
J	K	S	P	E	I	O	L	C	I	C	F	C	I	M
Z	W	O	B	R	W	O	R	D	O	Y	W	H	D	E
X	V	H	V	C	J	N	R	E	N	P	G	W	N	B
J	W	Q	E	R	A	A	H	M	L	Y	L	O	U	A
F	E	Z	B	E	M	K	U	U	Y	V	K	J	L	H
X	Y	R	O	D	S	F	J	O	Y	B	L	P	B	D
W	O	T	R	I	V	K	J	M	O	X	A	K	L	M
E	H	C	N	A	M	I	D	P	U	F	P	F	J	M

Search YouTube for 'Les sept jours de la semaine, Etienne' which is sung to the theme of *The Flintstones*.

Objectifs

- I know the days of the week off by heart

Récapitulatif

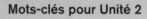

Mots-clés pour Unité 2

Bonne rentrée card

Greetings	Message	Signing off
Cher (m)	Bonne rentrée !	Amitiés
Chère (f)	Amuse-toi bien !	Ton ami
Salut	Bon courage pour la rentrée au collège !	Ton amie
Bonjour	On se fait des amis.	À bientôt
Coucou		Bisous

Dans la salle de classe
Le professeur

- Ouvrez vos livres
- Écrivez
- Travaillez avec votre camarade de classe
- Fermez vos livres
- Écoutez
- Regardez
- Répétez
- Je vais faire l'appel

Les élèves

- Je peux aller aux toilettes, s'il vous plait ?
- Qu'est-ce que ça veut dire ?

Mes affaires d'école

- une trousse
- une calculatrice
- un cahier
- un stylo
- une colle
- un livre
- un crayon
- une agrafeuse
- un cartable
- un feutre
- des ciseaux
- un iPod
- une clé USB
- un taille-crayon
- un portable
- une gomme
- un classeur
- un surligneur
- une règle
- un agenda

Mots-clés pour l'Unité 2

Parlons en classe

- Je peux emprunter …
- Oui, bien sur
- Tiens

- Merci
- De rien
- Non, désolé(e), je n'ai pas de …

- Ce n'est pas grave

L'alphabet en français

a = ah
b = bay
c = say
d = day
e = eh
f = eff
g = jhay
h = ash
i = ee
j = jhee

k = kah
l = el
m = em
n = en
o = oh
p = pay
q = koo
r = air
s = ess
t = tay

u = ooh
v = vay
w = doo-bluh-vay
x = eex
y = ee-grek
z = zed

On est quel jour aujourd'hui ? Aujourd'hui, on est …

- lundi
- mardi
- mercredi

- jeudi
- vendredi
- samedi

- dimanche

Bilan de l'Unité 2. *Checklist for Unit 2.*

Pour chaque objectif, choisissez votre émoticône.	😊	😐	😞
Listening			
I can understand simple classroom phrases and instructions from my teacher or classmate			
I can understand when someone asks me what something is			
I can understand my classmate when they ask me for a school item			
I can understand someone describing what is in their schoolbag and pencil case			
I can understand when someone spells something slowly			

Unité 2 : Au Collège

Bilan de l'Unité 2. *Checklist for Unit 2.*

Reading			
I can read labels of school items in French			
I can read a simple book list in French			
I can read a short infographic about school items in France			
Spoken production			
I can name the items in my pencil case and schoolbag			
I can spell my name in French			
I can name the days of the week			
I can say the alphabet			
Spoken interaction			
I can ask to borrow something from my partner			
I can ask my teacher a basic classroom question			
I can play *Jacques a dit*			
I can interview my partner about themselves and school			
Writing			
I can draw and label my school items			
I can make posters with classroom phrases			
I can write a card wishing someone *bonne rentrée*			

Discutez en classe. *Have a class discussion.*

- Look back over your Portfolio exercises. In which areas did you give yourself stars?

- Look at your wishes. Have any of these improved?

- What was your favourite part of Unité 2? Why?

- What did you least enjoy in Unité 2? Why?

- You completed many different kinds of activities in Unité 2. What kinds of activities were the best for helping you to learn? Why?

- Think about the next unit you will work on. What are you looking forward to learning more about? Why?

1. **Lisez les passages et répondez aux questions dans votre cahier.** *Read the extracts and answer the questions in your copybook.*

(A)

> Salut, je m'appelle Marwann. J'ai 12 ans et j'habite à Paris. Je parle français et arabe. Ma mère est tunisienne et mon père est français. J'aime le foot et la musique pop. Je n'aime pas le cyclisme.

1. How old is Marwann?
2. Where does he live?
3. What languages does he speak?
4. How does he know two languages?
5. What sport does he like?

(B)

> Bonjour ! Je m'appelle Chloé et je suis française. J'habite en Normandie. J'ai treize ans. Mon anniversaire est en janvier. C'est la rentrée et j'organise mes affaires d'école. J'ai mon nouveau cartable mais j'ai encore besoin de choses : un stylo rouge et un taille-crayon. Voici ma trousse et voici mes stylos bleus, ma règle, ma gomme, mes ciseaux et mes crayons.

1. Where does Chloé live?
2. How old is she?
3. When is her birthday?
4. Which two items does she still need to get for *la rentrée*?
5. Name three things she already has.

2. **Faites des recherches sur Internet puis répondez aux questions dans votre cahier.** *Research online, then answer the questions in your copybook.*

1. Find two pieces of information about Mont-Saint-Michel.
2. Name two foods for which Normandy is famous.
3. Name one region that borders Normandy.
4. Find two ways that people can travel from Ireland to Normandy.

3. (A) **Écrivez trois mots transparents que vous avez appris dans l'Unité 1.** *List three cognates that you learned in Unité 1.*

1. _____ 2. _____

3. _____

(B) **Écrivez les adjectifs au féminin puis traduisez-les.** *Write the feminine adjectives, then translate them.*

masculin	féminin	anglais
irlandais		
polonais		
canadien		
français		

4. (A) **Mettez les chiffres dans le bon ordre.** *Put the numbers in the correct order.*

trois, un, deux, quatre, cinq

_____ _____ _____

_____ _____

(B) **Remplissez les blancs.** *Fill in the blanks.*

Un, deux, _____, quatre, _____, six,

_____ huit, _____, dix

(C) **Comptez de trois en trois et remplissez les blancs.** *Count in threes and fill in the blanks.*

Trois, _____, _____

(D) **Comptez de deux en deux et remplissez les blancs.** *Count in twos and fill in the blanks.*

_____, quatre, _____, huit,

_____

5. (A) **Trouvez les bons pronoms sujets et entourez-les.** *Find the correct subject pronouns and circle them.*

1. Je / Tu / On _____ suis irlandais.

2. Nous / Vous / Ils _____ sont contents.

3. Tu / Vous / Elle _____ es en sixième.

4. Vous / Elle / On _____ êtes français.

5. Ils / Elles / Il _____ est sympa.

(B) **Remplissez les blancs avec la bonne forme du verbe *être*. Puis faites des phrases négatives dans votre cahier.** *Fill in the blanks using the correct part of the verb* être. *Then write the phrases in the negative in your copybook.*

1. Je _____ irlandais.

2. Vous _____ grand.

3. Ils _____ amusants.

4. Tu _____ française.

5. Nous _____ canadiens.

6. **Remplissez les blancs avec les mots de l'encadré.** *Fill in the blanks with the words in the box.*

(A)

| m'appelle | J'adore | Je | J'habite | J'aime | cool | J'ai |

Salut ! Je _____ Zoé. _____ 12 ans. _____ à Bray. _____ le chocolat et la musique. J'aime aussi le foot. _____ le cinéma. C'est _____ . _____ déteste le golf ! Ce n'est pas mon truc.

(B)

| J'aime | Salut ! | cool ! | parents | ans | mon truc |

_____ Je m'appelle Bertrand. J'ai 13 _____ et j'habite à Nantes. Mes _____ s'appellent Louis et Marie. _____ le cyclisme. J'adore le Tour de France. Le cyclisme est super _____ Je n'aime pas le ski. Ce n'est pas _____ .

À vous de jouer ! Unités 1 et 2

 7. Jeu de plateau. *Board game.*

You will need:

- A different coloured counter for each player
- A dice

Rules

- 2–5 players
- The youngest player rolls first, the second-youngest rolls second, etc.
- Roll the dice and move on that number of squares.
- Take the challenge on your square.
- If you give an incorrect answer, you miss a turn.
- The first player to reach 'Vous avez gagné' wins the game!

Astuces

Try to use as much French as possible during the game. Here are some useful phrases.

Commençons !	Let's begin!
À moi !	My turn!
À toi !	Your turn!
Lance le dé !	Throw the dice!
Avance d'une case !	Move forward one square!
Recule d'une case !	Go back one square!
Passe ton tour !	Miss a turn !

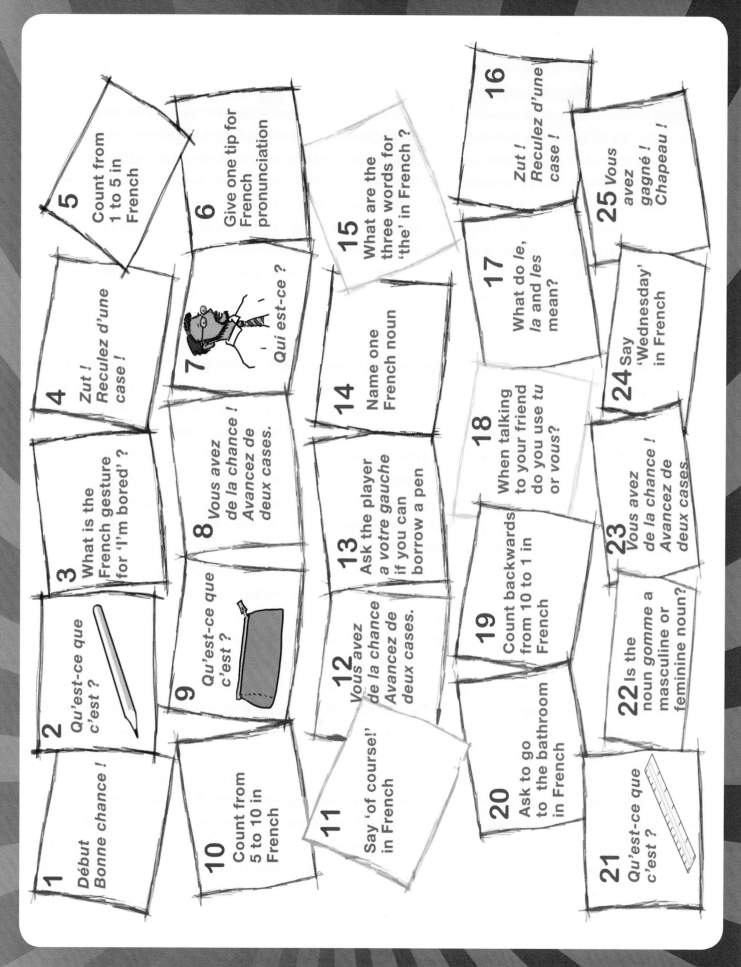

1 Début
Bonne chance !

2 Qu'est-ce que c'est ?

3 What is the French gesture for 'I'm bored' ?

4 Zut !
Reculez d'une case !

5 Count from 1 to 5 in French

6 Give one tip for French pronunciation

7 Qui est-ce ?

8 Vous avez de la chance ! Avancez de deux cases.

9 Qu'est-ce que c'est ?

10 Count from 5 to 10 in French

11 Say 'of course!' in French

12 Vous avez de la chance ! Avancez de deux cases.

13 Ask the player a votre gauche if you can borrow a pen

14 Name one French noun

15 What are the three words for 'the' in French ?

16 Zut !
Reculez d'une case !

17 What do le, la and les mean?

18 When talking to your friend do you use tu or vous?

19 Count backwards from 10 to 1 in French

20 Ask to go to the bathroom in French

21 Qu'est-ce que c'est ?

22 Is the noun gomme a masculine or feminine noun?

23 Vous avez de la chance ! Avancez de deux cases

24 Say 'Wednesday' in French

25 Vous avez gagné ! Chapeau !

8.

Une petite pièce de théâtre ! *A little theatre play!*

> Below is the script for a short play. Act it out in small groups. It's a great way to practise your new vocabulary. Audience members can take notes to help the actors improve on their pronunciation!

Présentation

C'est la rentrée au collège St Michael et les élèves sont en classe de français avec Madame Lefebvre. Ils pratiquent le nouveau vocabulaire pour parler français en salle de classe.

Liste des personnages

Audrey	Les autres élèves
Jean	Madame Lefebvre

Audrey : Bonjour, je m'appelle Audrey. Bonne rentrée !

Jean : Salut, Audrey. Je m'appelle Jean. Bonne rentrée à toi aussi.

Audrey : Merci, Jean.

Madame Lefebvre : Bonjour, tout le monde ! Je suis votre professeur, Madame Lefebvre. Bonne rentrée à tous.

Les élèves : Bonjour, Madame Lefebvre. Bonne rentrée à vous.

Audrey (à Jean) : J'aime Madame Lefebvre, elle est sympa. Jean, je peux emprunter un stylo, s'il te plait ?

Jean : Bien sur. Voici un stylo, Audrey. Tu as raison : Madame Lefebvre est sympa. On a de la chance.

Madame Lefebvre : Aujourd'hui on va parler français – et pas anglais – pendant la classe. Donc, écoutez et répétez les mots-clés avec moi.

Les élèves : Oui, madame.

Madame Lefebvre : Ouvrez vos livres.

Les élèves : Ouvrez vos livres.

Madame Lefebvre : Le « r » en français est différent, non ? Mais tu dis bien, Audrey.

Audrey : Merci, madame.

Madame Lefebvre : Et Jean … tu peux dire le « r » ?

Jean : « r »

Audrey : C'est bien, Jean !

Madame Lefebvre : Oui, c'est excellent. Vous avez un très bon accent français. Alors maintenant, répétez s'il vous plait : « Comment ça s'écrit ? »

Les élèves : Comment ça s'écrit ?

Madame Lefebvre : Super tout le monde ! Je suis très contente.

[Un peu après]

Madame Lefebvre : Et voilà, c'est fini pour aujourd'hui, merci. À demain !

Les élèves : Merci, madame – au revoir.

Audrey : On a musique maintenant, Jean ?

Jean : Oui, et j'ai oublié mon livre !

Audrey : Oh Jean, dépêche-toi !

Jean : Oui oui, j'arrive !

UNITÉ 3

Ma famille, mes animaux et moi

By the end of this unit you will

- Name the different members of your family
- Talk a little about your family
- Ask your friend about his or her family
- Name different pets
- Talk a little about your pet
- Use adjectives to describe people and pets
- Describe yourself and a friend
- Use the verb *avoir*
- Recognise and use possessive adjectives
- Write a short informal letter about yourself and your family.

Ex. 3.1 Ma famille

Écoutez le CD et entrainez-vous à bien prononcer le vocabulaire. *Listen to the CD and repeat the vocabulary to improve your pronunciation.*

Ma famille

- Mes parents
- Mon père, mon papa
- Ma mère, ma maman
- Mes grands-parents

- Mon grand-père
- Ma grand-mère
- Mon frère
- Ma sœur

- Mon fils
- Ma fille
- Mon petit-fils
- Ma petite-fille

- Mon oncle
- Ma tante
- Mon cousin
- Ma cousine

Prononciation

- In French, *ill*, as in *fille*, has an *eey(uh)* sound, not an *l* sound. We do not hear the *l* sound when we say the word *famille*.

- Be careful with the last consonant of French words. Usually, the last consonant is silent, e.g. *maman, cousin*. However, when an *e* is added in the feminine, you will notice that there is a change to the pronunciation, e.g. *ma cousine*.

- Pay attention to the word *fils*: we don't pronounce the *l* but we do pronounce the *s* here.

Objectifs

- **I can pronounce the *ill* sound correctly**
- **I know when to pronounce the final consonant**

Ex. 3.2 Ma famille

Écoutez le CD et entrainez-vous à bien prononcer le vocabulaire. *Listen to the CD and repeat the key words to improve your pronunciation.*

Ma famille

- L'ainé (e)
- Le cadet, le benjamin
- La cadette, la benjamine

- Mon beau-père
- Ma belle-mère
- Mon parrain

- Ma marraine
- Mon demi-frère
- Ma demi-sœur

Objectifs

- I can understand and name the different family members

Ex. 3.3 La famille

Reliez les images avec les descriptions. *Match the pictures of each family to the correct descriptions.*

(a) Je m'appelle Léo et voici ma famille. Je suis sportif, grand et sympa. Ma mère s'appelle Amélie, mon père s'appelle Vincent. J'ai une sœur et un frère. Mon frère s'appelle Lionel, il est le cadet. Il a cinq ans. Ma sœur s'appelle Vanessa, elle a douze ans. Mon grand-père habite chez nous. Il s'appelle Corentin. Il est très drôle et sympa.

(b) Je m'appelle Zoé. J'ai treize ans. Je suis bavarde et sympa. Ma mère s'appelle Maryse et mon père s'appelle Thomas. Ma mère a les cheveux noirs et les yeux marron. Mon père a les cheveux noirs et les yeux marron aussi. Je suis fille unique.

(c) Je m'appelle Guillaume. J'ai quatorze ans et j'ai un frère. Mon frère s'appelle David. Il a douze ans. Mes grands-parents s'appellent Julie et Daniel. Ils habitent à Nice, près de chez nous.

(d) Je m'appelle Laetitia et mon père s'appelle Pierre. Je suis petite et sportive. Nous habitons à Collioure. J'ai une sœur. Elle s'appelle Océane. Je suis la cadette.

Ex. 3.4 Vidéo

Deux jeunes parlent de leur famille. Regardez la vidéo et répondez aux questions en anglais. *Two young people describe their families. Watch the video and answer the questions in English.*

Agnès

1. How old is Agnès?

   _____

2. Where does she live?

   _____

3. How many brothers has she?

   _____

4. How many sisters has she?

   _____

5. What are her parents' names?

   _____

6. What is her aunt's name?

   _____

Jérôme

1. How old is Jérôme?

   _____

2. How does he describe his personality?

   _____

3. Where does he live?

   _____

4. How many brothers has he?

   _____

5. How many sisters has he?

   _____

6. What is his mum's name?

   _____

Un verbe irrégulier   Avoir – *to have*

We have already met an irregular verb, *être* in Unité 2. Now we will learn about the irregular verb *avoir*, which means *to have*.

Remember that irregular verbs do not follow a pattern and do not have set endings. With *être*, *avoir* is one of the most important irregular French verbs.

Ex. 3.5 Le Verbe *avoir*

Écoutez le CD et répétez le verbe *avoir*. *Listen to the CD and repeat the verb* avoir.

- J'ai
- Tu as
- Il a
- Elle a
- Nous avons
- Vous avez
- Ils ont
- Elles ont

 Ex. 3.6

Complétez avec la bonne forme du verbe *avoir* **ou le bon pronom sujet.** *Complete, using the correct parts of the verb* avoir *or the correct subject pronoun.*

J' _____	Nous _____
Tu _____	_____ avez
_____ a	Ils _____
_____ a	_____ ont
On _____	

 Ex. 3.7

Complétez les phrases avec le verbe *avoir*. *Complete the sentences, using* avoir.

Exemple : (I) _____J'ai_____ un stylo.

1. (You, familiar) _____ une gomme.

2. (We) _____ deux frères.

3. (He) _____ un cahier dans son cartable.

4. (They) _____ des crayons dans leur trousse.

5. (You formal) _____ une cousine ?

6. (I) _____ une sœur.

7. (She) _____ des cousins à Bordeaux.

8. Louise _____ une règle.

9. Thomas _____ un frère.

10. (They, masculine) _____ des stylos.

Objectifs

- I understand and can use the irregular verb *avoir*

Astuces

Inference is a useful strategy when learning a language: it means finding answers and understanding new words from clues in a text, and from knowledge you may already have about a topic. You will see how inference helps you with the following exercise on The Simpsons. The focus here is on the missing words, so having a prior knowledge about The Simpsons is a real help! Who would have thought that watching those cartoons would come in useful in school one day?

  Ex. 3.8 Les Simpsons

Écoutez le CD et complétez les blancs avec les mots de l'encadré. *Listen to the CD and fill in the blanks.*

Lisa: Je m'appelle Lisa. J'habite à Springfield aux États-Unis.

Je vous _____ ma famille.

Ma _____ s'appelle Marge et mon

_____ s'appelle Homer.

J'_____ une sœur et un frère.

Ma _____ s'appelle Maggie et

mon _____ s'appelle Bart. Bart

_____ drôle mais il n'est pas intelligent. Il adore faire

des bêtises. Il n'aime pas l'école mais moi, j'adore l'école et _____. J'adore le saxophone.

C'est mon truc. Maggie est la _____. Elle adore sa tétine.

Elle est mignonne mais elle ne parle pas. J'ai aussi deux _____.

Elles s'appellent Selma et Patty. Mon _____ est très vieux.

mère	père	est
la musique	grand-père	frère
cadette	ai	sœur
tantes	présente	

Ex. 3.9 Discutez en classe

When we read Lisa's paragraph in Ex. 3.8 we can see that it is more than just a sentence or two. Now look at the two paragraphs below: a short paragraph and a mid-length paragraph. Have a class discussion about which paragraph is better and why.

Short paragraph

Je suis Lisa. J'ai un frère. Mon frère, c'est Bart. J'ai une sœur. Ma sœur, c'est Maggie. J'ai des parents. Mon père, c'est Homer. Ma mère, c'est Marge. J'ai des tantes et un grand-père.

Mid-length paragraph

Je m'appelle Lisa. Je suis petite et j'ai les cheveux jaunes. Je suis intelligente et sympa. J'adore l'école et la musique. Le saxophone, c'est mon truc. Mon frère s'appelle Bart et il est drôle. Il adore faire des bêtises. Ma sœur s'appelle Maggie. C'est la cadette et elle est mignonne. J'ai aussi deux tantes et un grand-père.

 # Ex. 3.10 Les paragraphes

Now compare the short paragraph, the mid-length paragraph and the long paragraph (in Ex. 3.8). Fill in the grid below. Think about the ways that you can improve the sentences and the paragraphs that you write.

	Short paragraph	Mid-length paragraph	Long paragraph (CD)
Verbs What verbs does Lisa use?			
Information What information does Lisa give?			
Adjectives Does Lisa use adjectives? Which ones? Does she use them in the masculine and feminine?			
Sentence length Are Lisa's sentences short or long? What words does she use to make her sentences longer (e.g. *et*, *mais*)?			
Vocabulary Does Lisa use interesting vocabulary? Can you give examples of it?			

Objectifs

● I can recognise and list how to improve my sentences in French ☺ 😐 ☹

 **Ex. 3.11 Écrivez**

Dans votre cahier, écrivez un paragraphe pour décrire votre famille. Utilisez les stratégies apprises dans Ex 3.10. *In your copybook, write a paragraph to describe your own family. Use the tips you learned in Ex. 3.10.*

Objectifs

● I can write a paragraph to describe my family ☺ 😐 ☹

  Ex. 3.12 Vocabulaire

Écoutez le CD et entrainez-vous à bien prononcer le vocabulaire. *Listen to the CD and repeat the vocabulary to improve your pronunciation.*

 Je parle de ma famille

● Oui, j'ai une/deux/trois sœur(s).

● Oui, j'ai un/deux/trois frère(s).

● Non, je n'ai pas de sœurs.

● Non, je n'ai pas de frères.

● Je n'ai pas de frères et sœurs.

● Je suis fils unique. Je suis fille unique.

● Je suis l'ainé(e).

● Je suis le cadet.

● Je suis la cadette.

● Ma sœur s'appelle …

● Mes sœurs s'appellent …

● Mon frère s'appelle …

● Mes frères s'appellent …

● Mes parents s'appellent …

Objectifs

● I can recognise and answer a short question about my family ☺ 😐 ☹

  Ex. 3.13 Les entretiens

Lisez les entretiens avec des jeunes et répondez aux questions. *Read the young people's interviews and answer the questions.*

Audrey :	Clément, tu as des frères ou des sœurs ?	Clément :	Elle s'appelle Emma.
Clément :	Oui, Audrey. J'ai une sœur et un frère.	Audrey :	Comment s'appelle ton frère ?
Audrey :	Comment s'appelle ta sœur ?	Clément :	Il s'appelle Jake.

Michel :	Audrey, tu as des frères et sœurs ?	Audrey :	Mon cousin Jean habite à Rennes. Il a quinze ans.
Audrey :	Non, je n'ai pas de frères et sœurs. Je suis fille unique.	Michel :	Et où habitent tes cousines ?
Michel :	Tu as des cousins, Audrey ?	Audrey :	Mes cousines Laure et Sylvie habitent à Nice. Elles ont quatorze ans. Elles sont jumelles.
Audrey :	Oui, j'ai un cousin et deux cousines.		
Michel :	Où habite ton cousin ?		

Vrai ou faux ? *True or false?*	True	False
1. Clément has two sisters.		
2. Jake is Clément's brother.		
3. Audrey is an only child.		
4. Laure is Audrey's cousin.		
5. Audrey's cousin Jean lives in Nice.		

 Objectifs

- I can read and understand short interviews of people talking about their families ☐

 **Ex. 3.14 À deux**

À deux : posez les questions sur la famille à un(e) camarade et répondez à ses questions. Complétez la grille. *Talk with your classmate. Ask them questions and reply to theirs. Fill in the grid with your answers and theirs.*

Prononciation

Remember to follow the basic pronunciation tips!

- The last consonants in French words are not usually pronounced.

- If a word is long, break it up into syllables, and give each syllable the same amount of stress.

- The French *r* sound comes from the back of your throat.

- Speak with a French accent!

- Can you remember how to pronounce these words in particular? *Famille, cousin, cousine* and *fils*.

Des questions	Mes réponses	Les réponses de mon/ma camarade
Tu as des frères ?	J'ai …	
Tu as des sœurs ?	Je n'ai pas de…	
Comment s'appelle ton frère ?	Mon frère s'appelle …	
Comment s'appelle ta sœur ?	Ma sœur s'appelle …	
Comment s'appellent tes parents ?	Mes parents s'appellent …	
Décris ta mère/ton père/ta sœur/ton frère	Elle est …	

Ex. 3.15 Interévaluation

First, fill in the grid below for yourself, then work with a partner to provide each other with feedback on your performances in Ex. 3.14.

Words I knew really well	
Words I didn't know	
Words I need to pronounce better	
Words I pronounced really well	
My intonation	

Ex. 3.16 Les descriptions

Écoutez le CD et entrainez-vous à bien prononcer le vocabulaire. *Listen to the CD and repeat the vocabulary to improve your pronunciation.*

Les descriptions

- verts
- noirs
- bleus
- blonds
- bruns
- roux

- châtains
- marron
- longs
- courts
- bouclés
- raides

Ex. 3.17 Les adjectifs

Traduisez les adjectifs en anglais dans la grille. *Translate the adjectives and fill in the table. Use a dictionary to help you!*

	anglais
verts	
noirs	
bleus	
blonds	
bruns	
roux	

	anglais
châtains	
marron	
longs	
courts	
bouclés	
raides	

Objectifs

- I can read and recognise some adjectives

Ex. 3.18 Le blog de Florian

(a) **Lisez le blog de Florian et répondez aux questions.** *Read Florian's blog and answer the questions.*

Salut,

Je m'appelle Florian et j'ai quatorze ans. J'habite à Antibes, dans le sud de la France. Je suis français. Je suis bavard et sociable. Je suis grand, j'ai les yeux bleus et j'ai les cheveux noirs et courts. Nous sommes quatre dans ma famille: mes parents, mon frère et moi.

Mon frère s'appelle Lucas. Il a neuf ans. Il a les yeux verts et les cheveux bruns et bouclés. Il est drôle et sportif. Mes parents s'appellent Marc et Véronique. Ils sont sympas. Mon père a les yeux bleus et les cheveux noirs. Ma mère a les yeux verts et les cheveux bruns.

1. How old is Florian? _____

2. Where does he live? _____

3. How many people are in his family? _____

4. How old is his brother? _____

5. How does Florian describe his brother? _____

6. Describe Florian's father. _____

7. What colour eyes has Florian's mother? _____

(b) **Reliez les phrases.** *Match the sentences.*

Je m'appelle	s'appelle Lucas
J'habite	sympas
J'ai les	Florian
Mon frère	et sportif
Il est drôle	yeux bleus
Ils sont	à Antibes dans le sud de la France

Mon portfolio 3.1 : Le blog de ma famille

Faites cet exercice dans votre portfolio. *Do this exercise in your portfolio.*

Les adjectifs. *Adjectives.*

Adjectives make your written and spoken French much more interesting.

● Example 1: Bonjour, je m'appelle Florian. J'ai quatorze ans.

● Example 2: Bonjour, je m'appelle Florian. J'ai quatorze ans et je suis grand et sportif. J'ai les yeux bleus et les cheveux noirs.

Example 2 gives us much more information about Florian. Can you underline the adjectives used?

We have already learned that in French, when we want to use adjectives, they must agree with the noun they are describing.

● If the noun is masculine, the adjective must be masculine: *Il est grand.*

● If the noun is feminine, the adjective must be feminine: *Elle est grande.*

Usually, we just add *e* to make an adjective feminine. Can you remember what happens if the adjective already ends in *e*?

Adjectives must also agree in number. So if a noun is plural, then the adjective must also be plural. Usually we just add *s* to make an adjective plural.

● *Ils sont grands* (masculine plural)

● *Elles sont grandes* (feminine plural).

Masculine adjectives ending in −*x* do not change in the plural (e.g. *roux*).

Only a few adjectives do not change at all when they are used with feminine or plural nouns (e.g. *marron*).

In French, when we describe our hair and our eyes, they are always plural. Look at the vocabulary list for hair and eyes in Ex. 3.16. What letter do most of these words end in? What does this tell us about the adjective and the noun it is describing?

Ex. 3.19

With your partner, read back over the information on adjectives. Take turns in explaining it to each other.

Ex. 3.20 La personnalité

(a) **Traduisez les adjectifs dans la grille.** *Translate the adjectives in the table.*

(b) **Écrivez les adjectifs au pluriel.** *Write the adjectives in the plural.*

anglais	masculin	pluriel
	timide	
	drôle	
	bavard	
	gentil	
	sportif	
	paresseux	

(c) Write out the rules that you have learned so far about forming adjectives in French. In small groups, make one poster for each of these rules, using examples from the adjectives you have seen so far in Unité 3.

Prononciation

- When adjectives change their spelling, they also change their pronunciation slightly. The final consonant of French words is silent (e.g. *bavard*). However, when we add *e* at the end, we need to pronounce the final consonant (e.g. *bavarde*).

- Remember that the *ill* sound behaves differently (e.g. *gentille* has an *ee(yuh)* sound).

 ## Ex. 3.21 Les adjectifs

Choisissez la bonne forme de l'adjectif. *Choose the correct form of the adjectives.*

1. Sophie est bavard/bavarde/bavardes. _____

2. Luc est grand/grandes/grands. _____

3. Mélanie est sociable/sociables. _____

4. Enzo est gentille/gentilles/gentil. _____

5. Marc et Enzo sont intelligent/intelligents/intelligente. _____

6. Léa et Jean sont sportive/sportif/sportifs. _____

7. Zoé et Jean sont drôles/drôle. _____

8. Martin et David sont paresseux/paresseuse. _____

Objectifs

● **I can use adjectives in French** _____

Lisez les descriptions de gens célèbres et reliez-les aux photos. *Read the descriptions of the famous people and match them to the correct images.*

1. Je m'appelle _____. Je suis drôle et bavard. J'ai les yeux noirs. Je n'ai pas de cheveux. J'habite dans un ananas. Mon meilleur ami s'appelle Patrick. J'adore les méduses.

2. Je m'appelle _____. J'habite aux États-Unis, mais je suis anglais. Je suis petit et très drôle . Je suis acteur. J'adore Carpool Karaoke. Mes amis s'appellent Freddie, Jamie et Jack.

3. Je m'appelle _____. J'ai les cheveux roux et les yeux bleus. Je suis drôle et timide. Mon meilleur ami s'appelle Harry. J'adore la magie.

4. Je m'appelle _____. J'habite aux États-Unis. Je suis américain. Je suis grand et très intelligent . J'ai les yeux marron. J'ai les cheveux gris. Ma femme s'appelle Michelle.

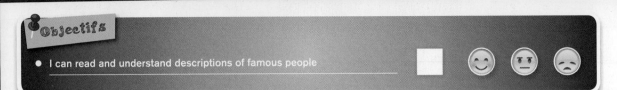

Objectifs

- I can read and understand descriptions of famous people ☺ 😐 ☹

Mon portfolio 3.2 : Je me décris

Faites cet exercise dans votre portfolio. *Do this exercise in your portfolio.*

Ex. 3.23 Vocabulaire

Écoutez le CD et entrainez-vous à bien prononcer le vocabulaire. *Listen to the CD and repeat the vocabulary to improve your pronunciation.*

Les mois

- janvier
- février
- mars
- avril
- mai
- juin

- juillet
- aout
- septembre
- octobre
- novembre
- décembre

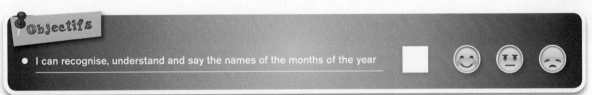

Objectifs

- I can recognise, understand and say the names of the months of the year ☺ 😐 ☹

Ex. 3.24

Ces fêtes se passent pendant quel mois ? *In what month of the year are the following festivals and events?*

1. _____

5. _____

2. _____

3. _____

4. _____

6. _____

7. _____

8. _____

Astuces

Remember that the days of the week and the months of the year take a small first letter in French, e.g. *lundi, janvier.*

L'adjectif possessif. *The possessive adjective.*

You may have noticed that there is more than one way of saying *my* in French:

- *Mon père*
- *Ma mère*
- *Mes parents.*

The word *my* is a possessive adjective. Notice how we use possessive adjectives in English:

- About a boy you will say: This is **his** brother and **his** sister.

- About a girl you will say: This is **her** brother and **her** sister.

French does it differently, changing the possessive adjective to **match the noun that follows**:

- About a boy: *C'est son frère (m.).*   *C'est sa sœur (f.).*

- About a girl: *C'est son frère (m.).*   *C'est sa sœur (f.)*

Remember that all nouns are either masculine, feminine, singular or plural. The word *my* can also be masculine, feminine, singular or plural.

- *Mon:* masculine singular words

- *Ma:* feminine singular words

- *Mes:* masculine and feminine plural words.

Ex. 3.25 Les adjectifs possessifs

Traduisez les mots dans la grille. *Translate the words in the table.*

 L'adjectif possessif

le	la	l'	les	anglais
mon	ma	mon	mes	
ton	ta	ton	tes	
son	sa	son	ses	
notre	notre	notre	nos	
votre	votre	votre	vos	
leur	leur	leur	leurs	

 # Ex. 3.26

With your partner, read back over the rules for possessive adjectives. Take turns in explaining them to each other.

Objectifs

● I can understand and explain possessive adjectives

 # Ex. 3.27

Choisissez le bon adjectif possessif. *Choose the correct possessive adjective.*

1. Mon/ma/mes père s'appelle Pierre. _____

2. Mon/ma/mes sœurs s'appellent Amy et Lucie.

   _____

3. Mon/ma/mes frère habite à Paris. _____

4. J'ai mon/ma/mes stylo dans mon/ma/mes trousse.

   _____

5. Votre/vos anniversaire est le deux septembre.

   _____

6. Marie adore son/sa/ses

   grand-mère. _____

7. Ton/ta/tes parents sont drôles. _____

8. Notre/nos cousin habite à Toulon. _____

9. Son/sa/ses tante habite à Biarritz. _____

10. Leur/leurs cousines adorent la musique.

    _____

Ex. 3.28 Le blog vidéo de Sophie

Regardez le blog vidéo de Sophie où elle parle de sa famille. Répondez aux questions en anglais. *Watch Sophie's video blog, where she talks about her family. Answer the questions in English.*

1. How old is Sophie? _____

2. When is her birthday? _____

3. Where does she live? _____

4. How many brothers does she have?

   _____

5. How many sisters does she have?

   _____

6. What are her parents' names? _____

7. What does Sophie like? _____

8. How does she describe herself? _____

9. How many aunts does she have? _____

10. How many cousins does

    she have? _____

● **I can understand a video of a person talking about themselves and their family**

  Ex. 3.29 Vocabulaire

Écoutez les trois jeunes qui parlent de leur famille et répondez aux questions en anglais. *Listen to the three young people talking about their families and answer the questions in English.*

	How old is this person?	Where do they live?	How many brothers and sisters do they have?	What month is their birthday?
Enzo				
Camille				
André				

Ex. 3.30 Les animaux de compagnie

Écoutez le CD et entrainez-vous à bien prononcer le vocabulaire. *Listen to the CD and repeat the vocabulary to improve your pronunciation.*

As-tu un animal de compagnie chez toi ?

- Oui, j'ai un …
- Non, je n'ai pas d'animal de compagnie chez moi.

- un chien
- un chat
- un hamster
- un poisson

- un cochon d'inde
- un cheval
- un lapin
- un oiseau

- un serpent
- une souris
- une tortue

Ex. 3.31

Écrivez le nom des animaux. Utilisez un dictionnaire. *Write the names of the animals. Use a dictionary to help you!*

1. _____

2. _____

3. _____

4. _____

5. _____

6. _____

7. _____

8. _____

Astuces

Remember: when we use adjectives in French, they agree with the noun they are describing. If the noun is masculine, the adjective must be masculine.

If the noun is feminine, the adjective must be feminine.

 Les adjectifs : la place et l'accord. *Adjectives: position and agreement.*

Colour adjectives, like most adjectives in French, go after the noun.

Example:

- *J'ai un chien noir.*

Some adjectives come *before* the noun. We will learn more about this later.

Examples:

- *J'ai un petit chien.*
- *J'ai une petite tortue.*

Usually, we add *e* to an adjective when it describes a feminine noun. However, some adjectives change their endings a bit more. What other changes in spelling do you spot in Ex. 3.32? (Hints: *n–nne* in *mignonne*, *x–sse* in *rousse*, *c–che* in *blanche*).

 # Ex. 3.32 Les adjectifs

Traduisez les adjectifs en anglais et complétez la grille. *Translate the adjectives into English and fill in the table.*

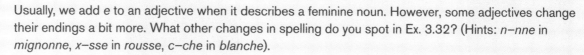

masculine	feminine	anglais
grand	grande	
petit	petite	
mignon	mignonne	
noir	noire	
blanc	blanche	
roux	rousse	
brun	brune	

 **Ex. 3.33**

With your partner, read back over the rules for the position and agreement of adjectives. Take turns in explaining them to each other.

  Ex. 3.34

Lisez les descriptions d'animaux célèbres et reliez-les aux photos. *Read the descriptions of famous pets and match them to the correct images.*

1. J'ai un grand chien marron avec des taches noires. Il adore les mystères. Mais il n'est pas très courageux ! Son petit frère s'appelle Scrappy. Il s'appelle comment ?

2. J'ai une chouette. Elle est petite et blanche. Elle est très belle et très intelligente aussi. Elle distribue des lettres et des cadeaux. Elle s'appelle comment ?

3. J'ai un escargot. Il est petit, rose et très mignon. Il ne parle pas. Je l'adore ! Il s'appelle comment ?

4. J'ai un gros chat orange. Il est drôle mais très paresseux. Il adore les lasagnes. Il s'appelle comment ?

A. _____

C. _____

 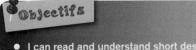

D. _____

B. _____

Objectifs

● I can read and understand short descriptions of pets ⬜ 😊 😐 ☹️

 Search YouTube for 'bande-annonce de *Comme des Bêtes*'. Before you watch the trailer for the film, can you guess what it is about?

 Astuces

A great way to improve your pronunciation skills is to read a French text and listen to a recording of it at the same time.

Ex. 3.35 La lettre d'Amélie

CD 1
T 37

Écoutez et lisez la lettre d'Amélie à son ami Luc. Répondez aux questions. *Listen to and read Amélie's letter to Luc. Answer the questions.*

(a) Remplissez les blancs. *Fill in the blanks.*

Paris, le 15 mai

Cher Luc, _____ Amélie. Mon professeur de français

Je _____ m'a donné ton adresse. Moi, j'ai treize ans. Mon anniversaire, c'est le

10 _____.

Tu as quel âge ? J'ai les yeux _____ noirs. J'ai une

et les _____ mais je n'ai pas de frère. Ma sœur

_____ s'appelle Julie: elle est gentille, _____ et

drôle. Elle adore la musique, surtout Fifth Harmony. Et toi, tu as des

_____ et sœurs ?

J'habite dans un appartement à Paris, près du Louvre, avec ma _____,

_____, mon _____. J'aime ma

ma sœur et ma _____ grand-mère Véronique, elle est sympa. Elle adore la musique.

Elle écoute tout le temps de la musique. Nous avons un

_____ chien noir. Il s'appelle Bruno.

Il est_____. Nous avons aussi un

_____ qui s'appelle Neptune. J'adore les

_____ ?

animaux. Tu as un _____

Je vais au collège à Paris. Je suis en sixième. J'aime mon collège. Tu

aimes l'école, toi ? Parle- moi de ton _____.

À bientôt,

Amélie

85

(b) **Vrai ou faux ?** *True or false?*

	True	False
1. Amélie has a brother.		
2. She is thirteen years old.		
3. Her birthday is in June.		
4. She lives with her mum and sister.		
5. Her grandmother loves dancing.		
6. Amélie has a dog and a fish.		

(c) **Reliez les débuts aux fins de phrases.** *Match the sentences.*

Je vais	m'a donné ton adresse.
Tu as	au collège à Paris.
Mon professeur de français	des frères ou des sœurs ?
Et toi, tu as	un appartement.
J'habite dans	quel âge ?

(d) **Traduisez.** *Translate.*

especially	
all the time	
I love animals	
Tell me about your school	

Lisez le passage à voix haute à votre camarade. *Read the letter out loud for your partner, practising your pronunciation.*

(a)   How does Amélie say 'Dear' in French?   (b)   How does she sign off her letter in French?

● I can read and understand a short letter about someone and his or her family and pets

Astuces

When you are writing an informal letter in French, a particular layout is used. Look at Amélie's letter in Ex. 3.35.

● Notice how Amélie has written the **place** she is writing from (the city) and the **date**. There is a comma after the city and a small first letter for the month of May.

● Her **greeting** is *Cher.* We will learn more later about starting letters in other ways.

● She **closes** her letter with *À bientôt* (See you soon/Hear from you soon).

● She **signs her name**.

● I know how to lay out an informal letter in French

Mon portfolio 3.3 : Une lettre pour décrire ma famille et moi

Faites cet exercise dans votre portfolio. *Do this exercise in your portfolio.*

Having a pen pal is a great way to practise your French and to learn about French culture! With **www.etwinning.net** you can 'twin' with a student in a school in France. You could share your video blog with them and ask them to create their own blogs to share with you!

Search online for **'www.tv5.fr A1 vidéo Moi, je suis'** to see a video about the funny ways in which families can be introduced to one another!

Récapitulatif

Mots-clés pour l'Unité 3

Ma famille

- Mes parents
- Mon père, mon papa
- Ma mère, ma maman
- Mes grands-parents
- Mon grand-père
- Ma grand-mère

- Mon frère
- Ma sœur
- Mon fils
- Ma fille
- Mon petit-fils
- Ma petite-fille

- Mon oncle
- Ma tante
- Mon cousin
- Ma cousine

- L'ainé (e)
- Le cadet, le benjamin
- La cadette, la benjamine

- Mon beau-père
- Ma belle-mère
- Mon parrain

- Ma marraine
- Mon demi-frère
- Ma demi-sœur

Je parle de ma famille

- Oui, j'ai une/deux/trois sœur(s).
- Oui, j'ai un/deux/trois frère(s).
- Non, je n'ai pas de sœurs.
- Non, je n'ai pas de frères.
- Je n'ai pas de frères et sœurs.

- Je suis fils unique. Je suis fille unique.
- Je suis l'ainé(e).
- Je suis le cadet.
- Je suis la cadette.
- Ma sœur s'appelle …

- Mes sœurs s'appellent …
- Mon frère s'appelle …
- Mes frères s'appellent …
- Mes parents s'appellent …

Les descriptions

- verts
- noirs
- bleus
- blonds

- bruns
- roux
- châtains
- marron

- longs
- courts
- bouclés
- raides

Les mois

- janvier
- février
- mars
- avril

- mai
- juin
- juillet
- aout

- septembre
- octobre
- novembre
- décembre

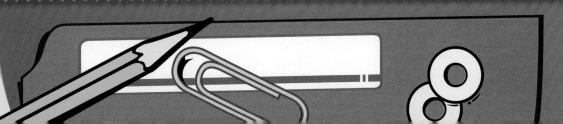

L'adjectif possessif

le	la	l'	les
mon	ma	mon	mes
ton	ta	ton	tes
son	sa	son	ses
notre	notre	notre	nos
votre	votre	votre	vos
leur	leur	leur	leurs

As-tu un animal de compagnie chez toi ?

- Oui, j'ai un …
- Non, je n'ai pas d'animal de compagnie chez moi.
- un chien
- un chat

- un hamster
- un poisson
- un cochon d'inde
- un cheval
- un lapin

- un oiseau
- un serpent
- une souris
- une tortue

Bilan de l'Unité 3. *Checklist for Unit 3.*

Pour chaque objectif, choisissez votre émoticône.	🙂	😐	🙁
Listening			
I can understand someone naming their family			
I can understand simple descriptions about someone's family			
I can understand someone telling me about their pet			
I can understand someone giving a simple description of their pet			
I can understand simple questions about family and pets			
Reading			
I can read a blog or a paragraph about someone's family			
I can read a description about someone's pets			
I can read short extracts about famous people, their families and their pets			
I can read a short informal letter about someone's family			

Spoken production			
I can say how many brothers and sisters I have			
I can talk about my family			
I can give a short description of the members of my family			
I can say if I have a pet			
I can give a short description of my pet			
Spoken interaction			
I can ask someone about their family			
I can ask someone about their pet			
I can respond with simple answers when asked about my family			
I can respond with simple answers when asked about my pet			
Writing			
I can write a simple description of my family			
I can write a blog describing my family and pets			
I can write a description of myself, my family and my pet, using adjectives			
I can write a letter naming and describing my family members and pets			

Discutez en classe. *Have a class discussion.*

- Look back over your Portfolio exercises. In which areas did you give yourself stars?

- Look at your wishes. Have any of these improved?

- What was your favourite part of Unité 3? Why?

- What did you least enjoy in Unité 3? Why?

- Think about the next unit you will work on. What are you looking forward to learning more about? Why?

UNITÉ 4

Chez moi

By the end of this unit you will

- Talk about where you live
- Describe your house
- Use the phrases *Il y a …/Il n'y a pas de …*
- Count from 1 to 30
- Describe how you help out at home
- Understand and use the irregular verb *faire*
- Describe your dream house
- Write a letter and a blog about where you live and how you help out at home
- Read advertisements of houses for sale
- Write your own advertisement of a house for sale and present it to the class.

Ex. 4.1 Ma maison et ma région

Regardez la vidéo et répondez aux questions. *Watch the video and answer the questions.*

1. Name two types of housing in France.

2. What is a holiday home called in French?

3. Who redesigned Paris in the 1850s?

http://www.education.vic.gov.au/languagesonline/french/French.htm is a website run by the Australian Department of Education with lots of fun activities to help you practise your French-language skills.

Objectifs

- I know what *résidence secondaire* means

Des prépositions. *Prepositions.*

A preposition is a small word that comes before a noun, pronoun or verb and connects it to another word. For example, in the sentence 'The book is on the table', *on* is the preposition. Other prepositions include *at*, *by*, *to*, etc.

In is a preposition of place. In French, there are a few different ways to say *in*:

- *dans*
- *en*
- *à la*
- *au*

You will need to learn certain phrases off by heart to ensure that you are using the right preposition.

Ex. 4.2 Vocabulaire

Écoutez le CD et entraînez-vous à bien prononcer le vocabulaire. *Listen to the CD and repeat the vocabulary to improve your pronunciation.*

Tu habites où ?

- J'habite à (name of town or city) en/ dans le (name of area)

- J'habite …

- dans une maison

- dans un appartement

- dans une ferme

- dans un village

- dans un lotissement

- à la campagne

- au bord de la mer

- en ville

- en banlieue

- près de …

J'habite à Celbridge en Kildare.

Objectifs

● I can understand where a house is situated

Ex. 4.3 Où se trouvent les maisons ?

Où se trouvent les maisons ? Écrivez les réponses dans votre cahier. *Where are these houses? Write the answers in your copy.* Exemple : La maison est au bord de la mer.

1.

2.

3.

4.

5.

6.

Objectifs

● I can describe where a house is situated

Astuces

Une chambre is the French for *a bedroom*. Remember what we learned about cognates in Unité 1? While we don't use the word *chamber* for *bedroom* in modern English, in previous centuries it was the English word for a bedroom!

Ex. 4.4

Des jeunes parlent de leur maison ou de leur appartement. Cochez la bonne case.
Listen to the four young people talking about where they live. Tick the grid.

	Une maison	Un appartement	Combien de chambres ?	À la campagne	En ville
Luc		✓			✓
Marie-Laure					
David					
Guillaume					

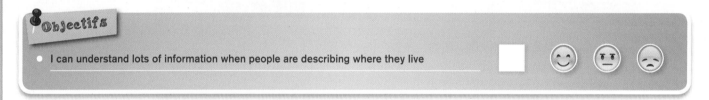

📌 **Objectifs**

● I can understand lots of information when people are describing where they live

😊 😐 😞

 **Ex. 4.5 À deux**

À deux : posez les questions sur là où vous habitez à un(e) camarade et répondez à ses questions. Complétez la grille. *Talk with your partner about where you live. Answer your partner's questions. Write your partner's answers in the grid below.*

Des questions	Mes réponses	Les réponses de mon/ma camarade
Tu habites où ?	J'habite à Kells.	
Décris où tu habites.		

📌 **Objectifs**

● I can pronounce the locations of houses

● I can ask my friend about where they live

● I can describe where I live

😊 😐 😞

Ex. 4.6 La Maison

Écoutez le CD et entrainez-vous à bien prononcer le vocabulaire. *Listen to the CD and repeat the vocabulary to improve your pronunciation.*

Dans ma maison, il y a …

- les pièces
- en haut
- le premier étage
- la chambre
- la cuisine
- la salle de bains
- le grenier
- en bas
- le rez-de-chaussée
- la salle à manger
- le sous-sol
- le salon
- le bureau
- le vestibule
- le jardin
- le garage
- les volets (m.)

Les maisons

- un appartement
- une maison de plain-pied
- une maison individuelle
- une maison jumelée

- chez moi
- chez toi
- chez Émilie

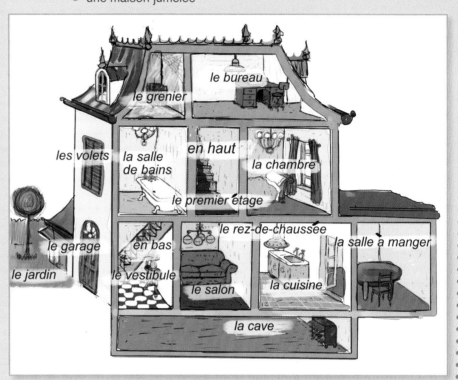

Prononciation

In French, the letters *ez* make an *[ey]* sound, e.g. *chez moi, chez Émilie.*

- The letters *eau* make an *[oh]* sound, e.g. *le bureau.*

Objectifs

- I can understand and name the rooms in a house

Il y a … Il n'y a pas de …

- Il y a … *There is/there are.*

- Il **n'**y a **pas** de … *There is not/there are not.*

- Il y a *un* jardin.   • Il y a *une* salle de bains.   • Il y a *des* volets.

- Il n'y a pas **de** jardin.   • Il n'y a pas **de** salle de bains.   • Il n'y a pas **de** volets.

  Ex. 4.7

Benjamin et Hannah parlent de leur maison. Écoutez le CD et répondez aux questions dans votre cahier. *Benjamin and Hannah talk about their homes. Listen to the CD and answer the questions in your copybook.*

Benjamin

1. Where is Benjamin's house?
2. What is on the ground floor?
3. What is on the first floor?
4. How many bedrooms are there in his house?
5. Does he have a garden?

Hannah

1. What is Hannah's home?
2. How many bedrooms are there?
3. Does she share her bedroom?
4. How many people are in Hannah's family?
5. How old is she?

Objectifs

- I can understand when people describe their homes and where they live

Ex. 4.8 La lettre de Manon à Niamh

Lisez la lettre de Manon à Niamh et répondez aux questions suivantes dans votre cahier.

Read Manon's letter to Niamh and answer the questions in your copybook.

Nice, le 18 octobre

Chère Niamh,

Merci pour ta dernière lettre avec les photos de ta famille. J'habite dans un grand appartement dans un grand immeuble à Nice près de la plage.

Mon appartement se trouve au cinquième étage. Est-ce que tu habites dans un appartement ou dans une maison ? Dans mon appartement, il y a huit pièces. Nous avons une très petite cuisine mais, heureusement, il y a une assez grande salle à manger. Il y a aussi deux salles de bains et trois chambres. Il y a aussi un salon où je regarde la télé. En France, beaucoup de maisons et d'appartements ont des volets. Nous avons des volets blancs. Nous avons aussi un ascenseur.

J'aime bien mon appartement et surtout j'adore habiter à Nice parce que j'adore la plage. Je t'envoie des photos de mon appartement. Est-ce que tu as un jardin ? Peux-tu décrire ta maison ?

Écris-moi vite

Manon

(a)
1. Where is Manon's apartment?
2. On what floor is Manon's apartment?
3. How many rooms are there?
4. What size is her kitchen?
5. How many bedrooms are there?
6. In France, lots of houses and apartments have shutters. True or false?
7. Is there a lift to Manon's apartment?
8. Why does Manon like living in Nice?
9. What two questions does Manon ask Niamh at the end of her letter?
10. Manon is including photos of her apartment in her letter. True or false?

(b) **Faites des paires.** *Match the pairs.*

1. Merci pour ta lettre
2. J'habite
3. Mon appartement se trouve
4. Dans mon appartement, il y a
5. Nous avons
6. Peux-tu

A. au cinquième étage.
B. huit pièces.
C. avec les photos de ta famille.
D. une très petite cuisine.
E. décrire ta maison ?
F. dans un grand appartement.

(c) **Utilisez les expressions ci-dessous et écrivez une description de votre maison/appartement.** *Use the phrases below to write a description of your home*

1. J'habite _____.

2. Mon appartement/ma maison se trouve _____.

3. Dans mon appartement/ma maison, il y a _____.

4. Il y a aussi _____.

5. Peux-tu _____.

Objectifs

- **I can read a letter about a person's house and where they live**
  _____

- **I can describe how to lay out a letter in French**
  _____

Mon portfolio 4.1 : Une lettre pour décrire là où j'habite

Faites cet exercice dans votre portfolio. *Do this exercise in your portfolio.*

Prononciation

The last consonant of French words is usually not pronounced. But some such as *c, r, f,* and *l* are pronounced. So be **CaReFuL**!

Be careful with your consonants as you practise saying the poem in Ex. 4.9!

Ex. 4.9 Un poème

Écoutez le poème et remplissez les blancs. Puis lisez le poème à voix haute pour ameliorer votre prononciation.
Read the poem out loud to practise your pronunciation.

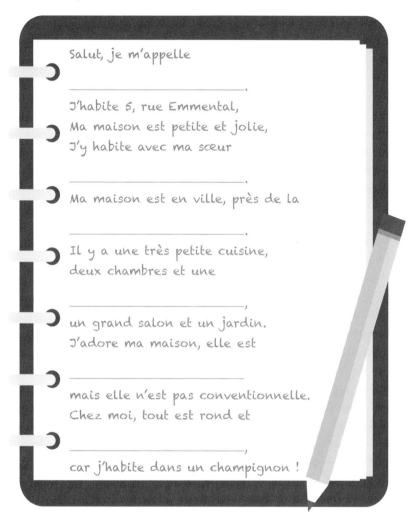

Salut, je m'appelle

_____.

J'habite 5, rue Emmental,
Ma maison est petite et jolie,
J'y habite avec ma sœur

_____.

Ma maison est en ville, près de la

_____.

Il y a une très petite cuisine,
deux chambres et une

_____,

un grand salon et un jardin.
J'adore ma maison, elle est

_____

mais elle n'est pas conventionnelle.
Chez moi, tout est rond et

_____,

car j'habite dans un champignon !

Objectifs

• I can read a poem with a good French accent

• I can pronounce the ends of words correctly

Ex. 4.10 Vocabulaire

Écoutez le CD et entrainez-vous à bien prononcer le vocabulaire. *Listen to the CD and repeat the vocabulary to improve your pronunciation.*

 Les nombres de 16 à 30

16 = seize	21 = vingt-et-un	26 = vingt-six
17 = dix-sept	22 = vingt-deux	27 = vingt-sept
18 = dix-huit	23 = vingt-trois	28 = vingt-huit
19 = dix-neuf	24 = vingt-quatre	29 = vingt-neuf
20 = vingt	25 = vingt-cinq	30 = trente

 Objectifs

● I can count from 1 to 30

 Ex. 4.11 Les adresses

Écrivez les adresses. *Write the addresses in your copybook.*

Exemple : ● Quelle est ton adresse ?   ● J'habite 20 rue Flaubert.

(a)

(b)

(c)

(d)

(e)

Objectifs

● I can give street names and house numbers

Ex. 4.12 À deux

À deux : posez les questions à un(e) camarade et répondez à ses questions. **Complétez la grille.** *Talk with your classmate. Ask them questions and reply to theirs. Fill in the grid with your answers and theirs.*

Des questions	Mes réponses	Les réponses de mon/ma camarade
Tu habites où ? Décris où tu habites.	J'habite …	
Décris ta maison.	Chez moi, il y a …	
Quelle est ton adresse ?	Mon adresse, c'est …	

Ex. 4.13 Interévaluation

First, fill in the grid below for yourself, then work with a partner to provide each other with feedback on your performances in Ex. 4.12.

Words I knew really well	
Words I didn't know	
Words I need to pronounce better	
Words I pronounced really well	
My intonation	

Objectifs

- I can ask my friend about where they live and ask them to give their address and describe their house

- I can answer questions about where I live and give my address and describe my house

Le château de Versailles, the Palace of Versailles, is 20 km south-west of Paris. It was built by King Louis XIII and enlarged into a royal palace by Louis XIV. In the years before the French Revolution, the French royal family lived at Versailles in great luxury and wealth. Nowadays, the *château* and gardens at Versailles are among France's most popular tourist attractions. Visit **http://www.versailles3d.com/fr** to take a virtual tour of the *château*.

Un verbe irrégulier   **Faire** – *to make/to do*

- The irregular verb *faire* has two meanings: *to make* and *to do*.

- When we want to describe the jobs we do around the house, we use the verb *faire*. See the examples in Ex. 4.15.

  Ex. 4.14 Le verbe *faire*

(a) **Écoutez le CD et répétez le verbe *faire*.** *Listen to the CD and repeat the verb* faire**.**

(b) **Traduisez le verbe *faire* en anglais.** *Translate the remainder of the verb* faire *into English.*

Je fais	I do/make.	I am doing/I am making.
Tu fais	You do/make.	You are doing/You are making.
Il fait	He	
Elle fait		
On fait		
Nous faisons		
Vous faites		
Ils font		
Elles font		

Prononciation

- We have learned that normally we do not pronounce the last consonants of words in French, e.g. *ils font*.

- However, when the last consonant is followed by an e, the consonant is pronounced, e.g. *vous êtes* .

Objectifs

- I understand and know the present tense of the verb *faire*

  Ex. 4.15

Écoutez le CD et entrainez-vous à bien prononcer le vocabulaire. *Listen to the CD and repeat the vocabulary to improve your pronunciation.*

Les tâches ménagères

- faire le repassage
- faire le ménage
- faire son lit

- faire la vaisselle
- faire la lessive
- faire la cuisine

   Ex. 4.16

Écoutez et complétez les phrases avec le verbe *faire*. *Listen and fill in the blanks using the verb* faire.

1. Je _____ un sandwich.

2. Vous _____ la lessive le samedi matin.

3. Tu _____ le ménage le weekend.

4. Daniel _____ son lit chaque matin.

5. Il _____ la vaisselle.

6. Ils _____ un gâteau délicieux.

7. Elle _____ son lit avant d'aller à l'école.

8. Nous _____ le repassage.

9. Elles _____ la cuisine chaque vendredi soir.

10. Tu _____ le repassage.

Ex. 4.17

Décrivez les images avec le verbe *faire*. *Describe the pictures, using the verb* faire.

A. Elle fait son lit.

_____

B. _____

C. _____

D. _____

E.

_____

F. _____

Objectifs

- I recognise and understand household tasks in French

 Astuces

We have met **three irregular verbs** so far. Can you name them? Why do we call them irregular?

It is important to keep revising these verbs to ensure that you know them off by heart. They are used a lot in spoken and written French!

 Ex. 4.18

With your partner, think about the three irregular verbs we have studied so far. Take turns in explaining what an irregular verb is. Discuss what each of the three irregular verbs means. Can you conjugate each one?

 **Ex. 4.19**

Complétez les phrases avec le bon verbe irrégulier. *Fill in the blanks with the correct irregular verbs.*

1. (suis/ai/fais) Je _____ en sixième.

2. (a/est/fait) Elle _____ la vaisselle.

3. (avons/faisons/sommes) Nous _____ la lessive.

4. (fais/as/es) Tu _____ un frère et une sœur.

5. (avez/êtes/faites) Vous _____ gentil.

6. (sont/ont/font) Ils _____ le ménage.

7. (font/ont/sont) Elles _____ deux sœurs.

8. (a/est/fait) Il _____ petit et bavard .

9. (suis/ai/fais) Je _____ le repassage.

10. (faisons/sommes/avons) Nous _____ un stylo dans notre trousse.

 **Ex. 4.20 Les régions et les départements de France**

Regardez la vidéo et la carte, puis répondez aux questions ci-dessous. *Look at the video and the map of the regions of France. Then answer the questions below.*

1. How many regions are there in France?

2. How many of these regions are overseas?

3. How are the departments listed?

4. True or false? Car owners in France can decide which department they want to display on their registration plate.

5. How many departments are there in France?

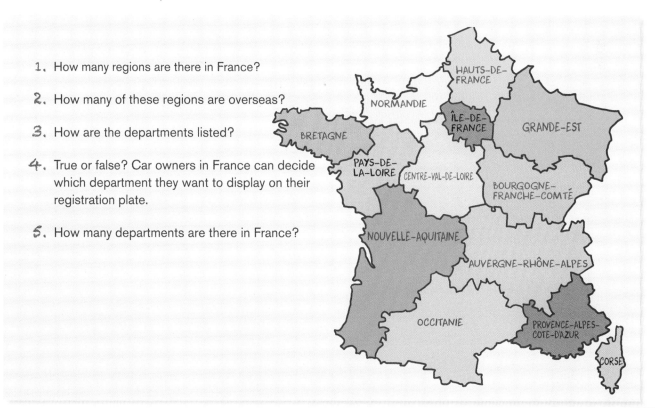

(b) Look at the registration plate below and search online to find which *département* this car comes from!

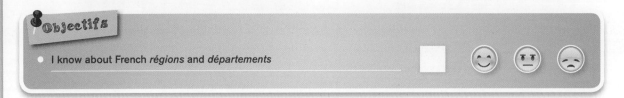

Objectifs

● I know about French *régions* and *départements*

Ex. 4.21 Vocabulaire

Écoutez le CD et entrainez-vous à bien prononcer le vocabulaire. *Listen to the CD and repeat the vocabulary to improve your pronunciation.*

Les points cardinaux / Les points de la boussole

- Le nord [N]
- Le sud-est [SE]
- L'ouest [W]
- Le nord-est [NE]
- Le sud [S]
- Le nord-ouest [NW]
- L'est [E]
- Le sud-ouest [SW]

Objectifs

● I can understand and name the points of the compass

Ex. 4.22 Les régions

Écoutez la description des régions de France. Répondez aux questions dans votre cahier. *Listen to the descriptions of regions in France. Answer the questions in your copybook.*

1. Where do French people prefer to holiday? _____

2. What town in the south of France is mentioned? _____

3. What are the *Gorges du Verdon*? _____

4. Name two regions of France where the countryside is similar to that of Ireland. _____

5. Where in France are these two regions located? _____

6. What is a popular sport on the west coast of France? _____

7. How long is the *Dune du Pilat*? _____

8. At what rate is it growing? _____

9. Discuss in class: Has anyone visited any of these regions in France? _____

CD 1 T 48

Ex. 4.23

Écoutez le CD et complétez la grille. *Listen to the CD and write your answers in the table below.*

	Il/Elle habite où? ville? village? bord de mer? campagne? banlieue?	Où est sa région? nord? sud? est? ouest?	Comment est sa région ? jolie? historique? intéressante? belle? petite? magnifique? verte? touristique?
Charles			
David			
Sylvia			
Maxence			
Laure			

- I can understand when people give short descriptions of their regions

Gites and campsites are popular for holiday accommodation in France. A *gite* is a holiday home: self-catering accommodation that you can rent. Visit **http://en.gites-de-france.com** to see *gite* for rent in France.

Campsites in France are very impressive. Many of them have swimming pools, restaurants and other facilities. Visit **http://www.siblu.fr** to see campsites in France.

Astuces

Conjunctions: developing your written and spoken French!

It is good to build your sentences using conjunctions or joining words, such as *mais, et* and *avec*.

- Here is an example of three short sentences in a row, without conjunctions:

J'habite dans une maison. Ma maison est vieille. Elle est confortable. Il y a une grande salle à manger. Il y a un grand salon. Il y a une télé immense dans le salon.

- Here is the same information, using conjunctions.

*J'habite dans une maison. Elle est vieille **mais** confortable. Il y a une grande salle à manger **et** un grand salon **avec** une télé immense.*

While both versions are correct, the second version shows that you can use conjunctions to build your sentences and make them more interesting.

- I understand how to improve my written and/or spoken French by using conjunctions

 **Ex. 4.24 À deux**

À deux : posez les questions à un(e) camarade et répondez à ses questions.
Complétez la grille. *Talk with your classmate. Ask them questions and reply to theirs. Fill in the grid with your answers and theirs.*

Des questions	Mes réponses	Les réponses de ma/mon camarade
Tu habites dans quelle région ?	J'habite …	
Tu fais quoi pour aider chez toi ?		

Ex. 4.25 Interévaluation

First, fill in the grid below for yourself, then work with a partner to provide each other with feedback on your performances in Ex. 4.24.

Words I knew really well	
Words I didn't know	
Words I need to pronounce better	
Words I pronounced really well	
My intonation	

Objectifs

- I can understand when someone describes their home, where they live and how they help out at home
- I can ask someone about their home, where they live and how they help out at home
- I can describe my home, where I live and how I help out at home

Les verbes en –er : –er verbs

In French there are three groups of regular verbs. Regular verbs end in either:

–er

–ir

–re.

A regular verb has the same stem throughout the verb, and follows a pattern with its endings. The good news is that **all regular verbs that end in –er follow the same pattern!**

To use an –er verb in the **present tense**, you need to do the following:

1. Knock the –er off the end of the verb: **regarder**

2. Now you have the stem: **regard-**

3. Add the correct ending for the subject pronoun, as shown in the table below.

Je -e

Ils/Elles -ent

Tu -es

– er verb endings

Vous -ez

Il/Elle/On -e

Nous -ons

Subject pronouns	Stem	Endings	to look
Je	regard	e	I look, I am looking
Tu	regard	es	You look, You are looking
Il	regard	e	He/It looks, is looking
Elle	regard	e	She/It looks, is looking
On	regard	e	One looks/We look, is/are looking
Nous	regard	ons	We look/are looking
Vous	regard	ez	You look/are looking
Ils	regard	ent	They look/are looking
Elles	regard	ent	They look/are looking

 Ex. 4.26 À deux

With your partner, think about regular verbs. What are the three groups? Take turns in explaining what a regular verb is and how we get the stem of a regular verb. List the endings for regular –er verbs.

 Ex. 4.27

Complétez la grille avec les bonnes formes des verbes réguliers. *Fill in the blanks with the correct parts of the –er verbs.*

- **First step**: get the stem of the verb.
- **Second step**: decide which endings go with each subject pronoun.

danser : *to dance*	jouer : *to play*	décider : *to decide*
Je danse	Je _____	Je _____
Tu _____	Tu joues	Tu _____
Il _____	Il joue	Il _____
Elle _____	Elle joue	Elle _____
On _____	On _____	On _____
Nous _____	Nous _____	Nous décidons
Vous _____	Vous _____	Vous _____
Ils _____	Ils _____	Ils _____
Elles _____	Elles _____	Elles _____

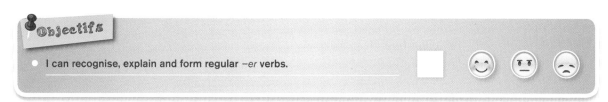

Objectifs

- I can recognise, explain and form regular –er verbs.   😊 😐 🙁

 Ex. 4.28 Les verbes en –er

Écoutez le CD et entrainez-vous à bien prononcer le vocabulaire. *Listen to the CD and repeat the vocabulary to improve your pronunciation.*

Des verbes en –er

décider	adorer	monter	aimer
frapper	écouter	aider	tomber
chanter	jouer	parler	
gouter	louer	rester	

 **Ex. 4.29**

Pouvez-vous deviner la signification des verbes de l'Ex. 4.28 en anglais ? *Can you guess the translations of the verbs you heard in Ex. 4.28? Do the verbs in French sound like verbs in English? Write the translations in your copybook.*

Prononciation

All except two of the different –*er* verb endings in the present tense are silent. Which two verb forms do not have silent endings? Look back to the verbs in Ex. 4.27 for a hint!

  **Ex. 4.30**

Écoutez et complétez les phrases avec le verbe à la bonne forme. *Fill in the blanks with the correct part of the verbs.*

1. Tu _____ (regardes/regarde) la télé avec ton frère dans le salon.

2. Vous _____ (danses/dansez) dans la chambre.

3. Elle _____ (écoutent/ écoute) son iPod dans sa chambre.

4. On _____ (goutez/ goute) le gâteau dans la cuisine.

5. Elles _____ (joue/jouent) au foot dans le jardin.

6. Je _____ (parle/parlons) à mon ami dans la salle à manger.

7. Ils _____ (restez/restent) dans la cuisine après le diner.

8. Nous _____ (aime/aimons) faire le repassage.

 Ex. 4.31

Décrivez les images. Que font-ils dans les différentes pièces ? *Describe the images. What are they doing in the rooms? Write the answers in your copybook.*

1.

2.

Exemple:
Il regarde la télé dans le salon.

3.

4.

 Objectifs

- I can choose and pronounce –er verb endings correctly

 Ex. 4.32

Utilisez des verbes réguliers en –er pour décrire ce que vous faites chez vous. *Use regular –er verbs to describe what you do at home.*

1. _____.

2. _____.

3. _____.

 Objectifs

- I can describe what I do at home using the present tense of regular –er verbs

 Ex. 4.33 Des agences immobilières en France

Regardez les annonces et répondez aux questions. *Look at the ads below and answer the questions.*

A. **Description générale**

Cette maison comprend six chambres sur deux niveaux, deux salles d'eau, une salle de bains, deux grands garages et une belle piscine.

Caractéristiques principales

- 243m² de surface habitable
- 12 pièces
- 6 chambres
- chauffage central au fuel
- 1 salle de bains
- 2 salles d'eau

€ 940 000

Nantes, Aux Portes De La Ville

B. Description générale

Cet appartement, d'une surface de 156 m², est situé au 3ème étage d'un immeuble avec ascenseur. Il y a une jolie vue sur l'église de Saint-Germain-des-Prés. Il y a une belle entrée, un salon avec balcon, une salle à manger, une cuisine bien équipée, trois chambres et deux salles de bains.

Caractéristiques principales

- 156 m² de surface habitable
- 6 pièces
- 3 chambres
- ascenseur

€ 2 780 000

Appartment de 156M² À PARIS 6ème

C. Description générale

Une jolie maison à la campagne. Au rez-de-chaussée, il y a un grand salon, une cuisine bien équipée et une salle d'eau.

En haut, il y a trois chambres et une salle de bains.

Au sous-sol, il y a deux chambres et une salle de bains.

Caractéristiques principales

- 166m² de surface habitable
- 6 pièces
- 5 chambres

€ 261 400

PLEYBER-CHRIST

	Vrai	Faux
1. La *résidence C* est à la campagne. Vrai ou faux ?		
2. La *résidence B* a quatre chambres. Vrai ou faux ?		
3. La *résidence A* a trois chambres. Vrai ou faux ?		
4. Which residence has a lift?		
5. Which residence has a swimming pool?		
6. Which residence has a basement?		
7. Which residence has the most rooms overall?		
8. Which residence has a large sitting room, kitchen and a washroom on the ground floor?		

Visit **www.immofrance.com** to see houses and apartments for sale in France and the different styles in each region.

 Ex. 4.34

Décrivez les maisons suivantes pour une agence immobilière. Lisez une description à voix haute à vos camarades de classe. *Write an estate agent's description for each of the houses below. Present one advertisement to the class.*

A.
- 2 bedrooms
- 1 bathroom
- balcony
- lift

B.
- upstairs: 4 bedrooms, 3 bathrooms
- downstairs: sitting room, kitchen, dining room, garage, pool

C.
- upstairs: 2 bedrooms, 2 bathrooms
- downstairs: sitting room, kitchen
- basement: 1 bedroom, 1 bathroom

Ex. 4.35 Le blog d'Ethan

Écoutez et lisez le blog d'Ethan. Puis répondez aux questions. *Listen to and read Ethan's blog. Answer the questions.*

Salut mes amis ! Je m'appelle Ethan.

J'ai treize ans et j'habite à Paris. J'habite dans un appartement dans le 6ème arrondissement. Mon appartement est assez grand. J'aime bien mon appartement et mon quartier est génial. Chez moi, nous avons trois chambres, deux salles de bains, une belle cuisine, un salon et une salle à manger. Mon ami Jules habite dans le même immeuble. Mon appartement est au deuxième étage, et Jules habite au troisième étage. C'est bien !

J'ai un frère mais je n'ai pas de sœur. Mon frère s'appelle Michel, il a 14 ans et il est sympa. Il adore la musique et il joue de la guitare. Ma mère s'appelle Camille et mon père s'appelle Tom.

À bientôt,

Ethan

(a) Répondez aux questions. *Answer the questions.*

(i) How old is Ethan? _____

(ii) Where is his apartment in Paris? _____

(iii) Does he like his *quartier*? _____

(iv) How many bedrooms are there? _____

(v) How many bathrooms are there? _____

(vi) Who is Jules? _____

(vii) Where does Jules live? _____

(viii) How many sisters does Ethan have? _____

(ix) What does Ethan like? _____

(x) What are Ethan's parents' names? _____

(b) Traduisez les mots suivants. *Translate the following words.*

(i) I live _____

(ii) Quite big _____

(iii) Nice kitchen _____

(iv) He is nice _____

(c) **Trouvez des exemples dans le texte.** *Find the following.*

(i) An example of a definite article _____

(ii) An example of a possessive adjective _____

(iii) An example of a masculine noun _____

(iv) An example of an *–er* verb _____

(d) **Reliez les phrases.** Match the phrases.

J'habite dans	je n'ai pas de sœurs.
Mon appartement est	un appartement dans le 6ème arrondissement.
Mon ami Jules habite	dans le même immeuble.
J'ai un frère mais	il joue de la guitare.
Il adore la musique et	assez grand.

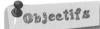 **Objectifs**

- I can read and understand a blog about a person's home and family ☐

 ## Astuces

In the *Mon portfolio Ex. 4.1,* you will write a letter about your house. Here are some tips to help you with written work:

- Make a plan/draft before you write.

- You have already written a letter to a pen pal on some of the topics that you will also cover here. Look back over your letter. Can you add any conjunctions or sentences to improve it?

- Writing is a redrafting process. This means that your first attempt or draft is a starting point only: you can always improve on it in a second attempt by redrafting it.

- When you have redrafted your work, it is time to proofread so that you can iron out any spelling or grammar mistakes. Have you got all of the accents on the right letters and going in the right direction? Proofreading your work will highlight simple mistakes so you can learn from them!

Récapitulatif

Mots-clés pour l'Unité 4

Tu habites où ?

- J'habite à (name of town or city) en/dans le (name of area)
- J'habite …
- dans une maison
- dans un appartement
- dans une ferme
- dans un village
- dans un lotissement
- à la campagne
- au bord de la mer
- en ville
- en banlieue
- près de …

Dans ma maison, il y a …

- les pièces
- en haut
- le premier étage
- la chambre
- la cuisine
- la salle de bains
- le grenier
- en bas
- le rez-de-chaussée
- la salle à manger
- le sous-sol
- le salon
- le bureau
- le vestibule
- le jardin
- le garage
- les volets (m.)

Les maisons

- un appartement
- une maison de plain-pied
- une maison individuelle
- une maison jumelée
- chez moi
- chez toi
- chez Émilie

Les nombres de 16 à 30

16 = seize	21 = vingt-et-un	26 = vingt-six
17 = dix-sept	22 = vingt-deux	27 = vingt-sept
18 = dix-huit	23 = vingt-trois	28 = vingt-huit
19 = dix-neuf	24 = vingt-quatre	29 = vingt-neuf
20 = vingt	25 = vingt-cinq	30 = trente

Les tâches ménagères

- faire le repassage
- faire la vaisselle
- faire le ménage
- faire la lessive
- faire son lit
- faire la cuisine

Les points cardinaux / Les points de la boussole

- Le nord [N]
- Le nord-est [NE]
- L'est [E]
- Le sud-est [SE]
- Le sud [S]
- Le sud-ouest [SW]
- L'ouest [W]
- Le nord-ouest [NW]

Des verbes en –er

- décider
- frapper
- chanter
- gouter
- adorer

- écouter
- jouer
- louer
- monter
- aider

- parler
- rester
- aimer
- tomber

Bilan de l'Unité 4. *Checklist for Unit 4.*

Pour chaque objectif, choisissez votre émoticône.	🙂	😐	🙁
Listening			
I can understand people telling me where they live			
I can understand when people give simple descriptions of their homes			
I can understand people telling me about household chores and activities			
I can understand when people tell me their address			
Reading			
I can read about a blog about a person's home			
I can read a poem in French			
I can read street names			
I can read door numbers in French			
I can read a short description about a person's home			
I can read a short description about how people help out at home			
I can read short advertisements from a French estate agent			
Spoken production			
I can ask someone where they live			
I can ask someone about their home			
I can ask someone how they help out at home			
I can ask someone their address			
I can say where I live			

Unité 4 : Chez moi

I can describe my house			
I can say my address			
I can pronounce the names of some regions in France			
I can count to 30			
I can pronounce some street names			
I can pronounce household tasks and activities			
I can present a simple advertisement of a house for sale			
Spoken interaction			
I can name the rooms in my house			
I can name some of the regions on a map of France			
Writing			
I can write a short blog about my house			
I can write about how I help out at home			
I can write a simple advertisement of a house for sale			
I can write a letter to a penpal, describing my home and where I live			

Discutez en classe. Have a class discussion.

- Look back over your Portfolio exercises. In which areas did you give yourself stars?

- Look at your wishes. Have any of these improved?

- What was your favourite part of Unité 4? Why?

- What did you least enjoy in Unité 4? Why?

- Have you found any new ways to help you learn French?

- Think about the next unit you will work on. What are you looking forward to learning more about? Why?

1. **Lisez le passage et répondez aux questions dans votre cahier.** *Read the extract and answer the questions in your copybook.*

> Bonjour, je m'appelle Jean-Luc. Je suis belge et j'habite à Bruxelles. J'ai treize ans. J'ai les yeux bleus et les cheveux blonds. Nous sommes cinq dans ma famille : mes parents, mes deux soeurs et moi. Mes sœurs s'appellent Chantal et Caroline. Chantal a vingt ans. Caroline a seize ans. Chantal a les cheveux noirs et raides. Elle a les yeux bleus. Elle est drôle et très intelligente. Caroline a les cheveux noirs et raides aussi. Elle a les yeux verts. Elle est très sportive. Mes parents sont sociables et sympas. J'adore le sport. J'aime Arsenal. Je déteste le golf !

1. In what city does Jean-Luc live?

2. How many people are in his family?

3. How old is Caroline?

4. How does Jean-Luc describe Chantal?

5. What sport does Jean-Luc like?

2. **Faites des recherches sur Internet puis répondez aux questions dans votre cahier.** *Research online, then answer the questions in your copybook.*

1. Belgium is a francophone country. What does 'francophone' mean?

2. What languages are spoken in Belgium?

3. How is Brussels connected with the EU?

4. What countries border Belgium?

5. Hergé was a famous Belgian cartoonist. What well-known character did Hergé create?

3. **(A)** **Choisissez la bonne forme du verbe *être*.** *Choose the correct part of the verb* être.

1. J' a/as/ai deux sœurs et un frère.

2. Nous ont/avons/as un chat noir et un chien marron.

3. Elle as/a/ai un stylo dans sa trousse.

4. Vous ont/as/avez un frère et pas de sœurs.

5. Ils a/avons/ont une souris et un serpent.

(B) **Complétez la grille avec les adjectifs.** *Fill in the table with the adjectives.*

verte	brune	bouclés
noirs	rouges	gentille
bleu	long	
blonds	courte	

masculin	féminin	m/f pluriel

(C) **Dans votre cahier, écrivez trois phrases pour décrire les jeunes: sur les images.** *In your copybook, write three phrases to describe the person in each picture.*

(D) **Soulignez le bon adjectif possessif.** *Underline the correct possessive adjective.*

1. Mon/Ma/Mes sœurs sont gentilles.

2. Ton/Ta/Tes frère s'appelle Josh.

3. Son/Sa/Ses amis s'appellent Emma et Jean.

4. Ton/Ta/Tes tantes ont deux grands chiens.

5. Marie aime son/sa/sess petit hamster.

(E) **Reliez les traductions.** *Match the translations.*

français	anglais		
1. Mes stylos	(a) His book	1	b
2. Ta sœur	(b) My pens		
3. Leurs amis	(c) Their friends		
4. Notre chien	(d) Her chair		
5. Votre école	(e) Our dog		
6. Son livre	(f) Your sister		
7. Sa chaise	(g) Your school		

(F) **Choisissez la bonne préposition.** *Choose the correct preposition.*

1. J'habite à la/en/dans une ferme.

2. Elle habite en/à la/dans banlieue.

3. Nous habitons en/dans/au bord de la mer.

4. Ils habitent au/à la/en campagne.

5. Tu habites en/à/dans le village.

(G) **Écrivez trois phrases pour décrire ces maisons.** *Write three sentences to describe these houses, using the phrases* Il y a *and* Il n'y a pas de.

Exemple : Chez les Dupont, il y a un garage.

Chez les Dupont

Chez les Martin

(H) **Complétez les phrases avec la bonne forme du verbe *faire*, puis traduisez les phrases.**
Complete the sentences with the correct part of the verb faire. *Then translate the sentences.*

Je _____ mon lit le matin.	faites/fait/fais	I make my bed in the morning.
Il _____ le repassage le weekend.	faisons/fait/fais	
Elles _____ la lessive le samedi.	faites/font/faisons	
Nous _____ nos devoirs après l'école.	font/fait/faisons	
Vous _____ le ménage chez vous.	faites/font/fais	

(I) **Lisez les indices et remplissez la grille de mots croisés.** *Read the clues and fill in the crossword.*

Horizontalement

2. Nous (aimer) la nouvelle maison.
5. Elle (chanter) dans la chorale.
7. Vous (parler) au professeur.
9. Elle (jouer) au foot samedi matin.

Verticalement

1. Ils (louer) un appartement en ville.
3. Tu (frapper) à la porte avant d'entrer.
4. Ils (écouter) de la musique pop.
6. Nous (aider) nos amis avec leurs devoirs.
8. Je (regarder) la télé le soir.

À vous de jouer !
Unités 3 et 4

✏️ **4.** **Complétez la grille.** *Fill in the table. Remember to use complete sentences!*

Comment vous appelez-vous ?	Je m'appelle
Vous avez quel âge ?	
Décrivez-vous.	
Vous avez des frères et sœurs ?	
Vous avez des animaux de compagnie ?	
Où habitez-vous ?	
Décrivez votre maison.	

5. Jeu de plateau. *Board game.*

You will need:

- A different coloured counter for each player
- A dice

Rules

- 2–5 players
- The youngest player rolls first, the second-youngest rolls second, etc.
- Roll the dice and move on that number of squares.
- Take the challenge on your square.
- If you give an incorrect answer, you miss a turn.
- The first player to reach 'Vous avez gagné' wins the game!

 Astuces

Try to use as much French as possible during the game. Here are some useful phrases.

Commençons !	Let's begin!
À moi !	My turn!
À toi !	Your turn!
Lance le dé !	Throw the dice!
Avance d'une case !	Move forward one square!
Recule d'une case !	Go back one square!
Passe ton tour !	Miss a turn !

1 Début !
Bonne chance !

2 Qu'est-ce que c'est ?

3 Où habitez-vous ?

4 Zut !
Reculez d'une case !

5 Count backwards from 10 to 1 in French

6 Give one tip for French pronunciation

7 Qu'est-ce que c'est ?

8 Vous avez de la chance !
Avancez de deux cases

9 Que fait-elle ?

10 Name the points of the compass in French

11 What is the Dune du Pilat ?

12 Vous avez de la chance !
Avancez de deux cases.

13 Vous avez des animaux de compagnie ?

14 Vous avez des sœur ?

15 What are the three words for 'the' in French ?

16 Zut !
Reculez d'une case !

17 Vous avez les yeux de quelle couleur ?

18 List the months of the year in French

19 Vous avez les cheveux de quelle couleur ?

20 Vous avez des frères ?
Comment ils s'appellent ?

21 Qu'est-ce que c'est ?

22 What are the Gorges du Verdon?

23 Vous avez de la chance !
Avancez de deux cases.

24 Vous avez quel âge ?

25 Vous avez gagné !
Chapeau !

6. Une petite pièce de théâtre ! *A little theatre play!*

> Below is the script for a short play. Act it out in small groups. It's a great way to practise your new vocabulary. Audience members can take notes to help the actors improve on their pronunciation!

Présentation

Il y a un nouveau chien chez les Martin. C'est l'anniversaire de Claire, la fille de Monsieur et Madame Martin. Ils lui ont offert un chien pour son anniversaire.

Liste des personnages

- Claire
- Emma
- Madame Martin
- Monsieur Martin
- Brownie, le nouveau chien

La scène se passe chez les Martin, dans la cuisine.

Madame Martin :

Bon anniversaire, ma petite !

Claire : Merci, maman. Oh … un cadeau pour moi ?!

Monsieur Martin :

Oui – bon anniversaire, chérie.

Claire : Ce n'est pas vrai ! Un chien ? Qu'il est mignon ! Je l'adore !

Emma : Claire, tu as de la chance – il est trop mignon ! Comment il s'appelle ?

Claire : Je ne sais pas encore. Il est marron et petit ... Peut-être ... Brownie ?

Emma : Oui, j'aime bien ça ! Bon – c'est Brownie. C'est parfait.

Monsieur Martin, Madame Martin :

Bonjour, Brownie !

Brownie : *Ouaf ouaf !*

Ouaf ouaf !

UNITÉ 5

Mon temps libre

By the end of this unit you will

- Talk about sports
- Know about the verbs *jouer à* and *faire de*
- Know about the preposition *depuis*
- Write a blog about your hobbies and sports
- Tweet about your sports day
- Learn about *–ir* verbs
- Be able to give your opinion in a group about sports and hobbies
- Learn the irregular verb *aller*
- Describe the weather and name the seasons
- Talk about what you do in different weathers
- Present a simple weather forecast

Ex. 5.1 La Vie en France

Regardez la vidéo et répondez aux questions. *Watch the video and answer the questions.*

1. Name three sporting events that take place in France.

2. What is the distance covered in the Tour de France race?

3. Where does it always finish?

4. Name two famous French sportspeople.

5. Where is the Stade de France?

6. What is the main aim of the game of *pétanque*?

7. Name the highest mountain in France.

8. Name a popular ski resort in France.

9. Who reached the final of the Euros 2016?

Objectifs

- I know about sports in France

Ex. 5.2 Vocabulaire

Écoutez le CD et entrainez-vous à bien prononcer le vocabulaire. *Listen to the CD and repeat the vocabulary to improve your pronunciation.*

Les sports

- le foot
- le rugby
- la pétanque/les boules
- le tennis
- le ping-pong
- le hockey
- le basket
- le golf

Astuces

Many French words for sports are very similar to the English words. Remember how we can use cognates to figure out the meanings of words. What sports can you guess from the cognates in the list?

Ex. 5.3 Les sports

Devinez les sports. *Guess the sports.*

- le tennis
- le golf
- la pétanque
- le ping-pong
- le rugby
- le basket
- le hockey
- le foot

Objectifs

- I can read and pronounce with a French accent the key words for sports
- I can recognise and understand the names of some sports

Ex. 5.4

Lisez les infographies et puis répondez aux questions dans votre cahier. *Read the infographics and answer the questions in your copybook.*

Les événements sportifs qu'elles préfèrent suivre :

Les Jeux olympiques 28% Roland Garros 14%

La Coupe du monde de Football 11%

Prêt, feu, partez !

1 Française sur 2 fait du sport entre ami(e)s

1 Française sur 2 déclare avoir un niveau avancé en sport

65% des Françaises font du sport 2 à 3 fois par semaine

Focus jeux olympiques

66% des Françaises vont suivre les JO

Top 5 des sports pratiqués :

Course à pied 17% Gym 17% Natation 14%

Vélo 13% Danse 10%

Ce qu'elles préfèrent dans cette compétition :

L'athlétisme

La gymnastique

Les sports aquatiques

23%

20% 19%

1. Which is the sporting event with the highest percentage of French women followers?

2. Sixty-five per cent of French women do sport three times a week. True or false?

3. What is the most popular sport for women in France?

4. What percentage of the French population do cycling?

5. What is the favourite Olympic sport of French women?

Objectifs

- I can read and understand some information about sports in France ☺ 😐 ☹

Jouer – *to play*

- *Jouer* is a regular –*er* verb

- With your partner, explain how we find the stem of an –*er* verb and what the –*er* endings are. Then translate the verb in the grid below.

Je joue	I play, I am playing
Tu joues	
Il joue	
Elle joue	
On joue	
Nous jouons	
Vous jouez	
Ils jouent	
Elles jouent	

Jouer à

When we talk about sports we use the verb *jouer* with the preposition *à*.

The preposition *à* changes depending on the gender (masculine/feminine) and number (singlular/plural) of the sport.

We use:

> *à la* for feminine sports = *Je joue à la pétanque*
>
> *au* for masculine sports = *Je joue au tennis*
>
> *aux* for plural sports = *Je joue aux boules*

- I can understand and explain the grammar rule behind the preposition *à* with *jouer*. _____

 Ex. 5.5

With your partner, read back over the explanation of the grammar rule for the verb *jouer* with the preposition à. *Think about the rule and take turns in explaining it to each other.*

Objectifs

- I can understand and explain the grammar rule behind the verb *jouer* and the preposition *à*

 Ex. 5.6 Jouer et la préposition à

Complétez les phrases avec la bonne forme de la préposition à. *Fill in the blanks with the correct preposition.*

1. Je joue _____ (au/aux) golf.

2. Tu joues _____ (au/aux) boules.

3. Elle joue _____ (au/aux) foot.

4. Nous jouons _____ (à la/au) basket.

5. Vous jouez _____ (au/à la) rugby.

Objectifs

- I can use the preposition *à* correctly with the verb *jouer* in a sentence to describe the sports I play _____

Ex. 5.7

Des jeunes parlent de leur sport préféré. *Listen to three young people talking about the sports they like.*

(a) **Écoutez le CD et remplissez les blancs.** *Listen to the CD and fill in the blanks.*

(b) **Répondez aux questions dans votre cahier.** *Answer the questions in your copybook.*

Emma : Moi, _____ le golf. Je _____ au golf au terrain de golf le _____ avec mes amis. C'est convivial et amusant.

Enzo : J'aime _____. Je joue au foot chaque _____ avec mes amis et je m'entraine avec mon équipe le _____ soir. Nous jouons un match de foot chaque samedi. Mon équipe s'appelle Tours Sportif. Le terrain de foot est près de chez _____. J'adore le foot et je regarde les matchs à la _____. Cette année, j'ai regardé l'Euro.

Lola : Moi, j'adore le _____. Je joue au tennis chaque mercredi. Le _____ de tennis est en ville. J'aime aussi regarder le tennis à la télé : Wimbledon et Roland-Garros, c'est _____. Je me passionne pour le tennis.

1. When does Emma play golf?
2. Why does she play golf?
3. When does Enzo train?
4. What did he watch on TV this year?
5. What does Lola do on Wednesdays?
6. Does she like to watch tennis on TV?
7. What does she think of Wimbledon?
8. Translate:

with my friends	
the golf course	
every evening	

134

I train with my team	
the football pitch	
the tennis court	
I'm mad about tennis	

Objectifs

- I can understand when I hear young people talk about their sporting activities ☐ 😊 😐 ☹

Astuces

The word *terrain* is used in different translations when we are talking about sports, e.g. *terrain de foot* is a football pitch. Can you remember any other translations we've seen so far? When learning a language, it's important to keep an open mind as we try to get a clear translation: we don't always get a 'word for word' translation or a direct swap of one French word for one English word!

Ex. 5.8 À deux

À deux : posez les questions sur le sport à un(e) camarade et répondez à ses questions. Complétez la grille. *Talk with your partner about sports. Answer your partner's questions. Write your partner's answers in the grid below.*

Questions	Mes réponses	Les réponses de ma/mon camarade
Tu aimes le sport ?	Oui, j'aime … Non je n'aime pas …	
Tu joues à quoi?	Je joue à la/au/aux …	
C'est quoi ton sport préféré ?	Mon sport préféré, c'est le/la/les …	
Pourquoi ?	Parce que c'est …	

Ex. 5.9 Interévaluation

First, fill in the grid below for yourself, then work with a partner to provide each other with feedback on your performances in Ex. 5.8.

Words I knew really well	
Words I didn't know	
Words I need to pronounce better	
Words I pronounced really well	
My intonation	

 Objectifs

- I can ask simple questions and answer simple questions about playing sports

  CD 2 T 4

Ex. 5.10 Vocabulaire

Écoutez le CD et entrainez-vous à bien prononcer le vocabulaire. *Listen to the CD and repeat the vocabulary to improve your pronunciation.*

 Des sports individuels

- le cyclisme
- l'alpinisme
- l'escalade
- la planche à voile
- la natation
- le patin à glace
- le patinage

- l'athlétisme
- l'équitation
- le ski
- le ski nautique
- le canoë
- la pêche
- la plongée

- la voile
- le judo
- la course à pied

● I can pronounce the key words for sports with a French accent.

Le verbe *faire* et les sports

We already know about the verb *faire*, which means to make or do.

In French, when we talk about sports we can use the verb *faire* with the preposition *de*. We do this in English too:

- I play basketball.

- I do climbing.

The guideline in French is that we use:

- *jouer à* for team sports

- *faire de* for individual sports.

Can you fill in the blanks for the verb *faire* in the table below?

Je	
	fais
Il	
Elle	
	fait
	faisons
Vous	
Ils	
	font

The preposition *de* changes depending on the gender (masculine/feminine) and number (singular/plural) of the sport. We use:

- *de la* for feminine sports = *Je fais de la voile.*

- *du (de + le)* for masculine sports = *Je fais du judo.*

- *des (de + les)* for plural sports = *Je fais des sports extrêmes.*

Ex. 5.11 *Faire et la préposition de*

With your partner, read back over the explanation of the grammar rule about the verb *faire* with the preposition *de*. Think about the rule and take turns in explaining it to each other.

Objectifs

● I can understand and explain the preposition *de*

 # Ex. 5.12

Complétez les phrases avec la bonne forme de la préposition *de*. *Fill in the blanks with the correct preposition.*

1. Je fais _____ (de la/du) ski nautique.

2. Tu fais _____ (du/de la) natation.

3. Vous faites _____ (des/de la) sports extrêmes.

4. Nous faisons _____ (de l'/de la) alpinisme.

5. Il fait _____ (de l'/de la) course à pied.

Objectifs

● I can use the preposition *de* with the verb *faire*

Ex. 5.13 Vocabulaire

Écoutez le CD et écrivez les noms de sports au bon endroit dans le tableau. *Listen to the CD and use the nouns to fill in the grid. Use a dictionary to help you.*

- la planche à voile
- la pétanque
- le ping-pong
- le canoë
- le golf
- le rugby
- l'athlétisme
- la pêche
- le basket
- le hockey
- le tennis
- le ski
- la voile

- la natation
- l'équitation
- les boules
- l'alpinisme
- l'aïkido
- l'escalade
- le cyclisme
- le patinage
- le judo
- le ski nautique
- la plongée
- le foot
- le patin à glace

Masculin	Féminin	Pluriel

 **Ex. 5.14**

Pour quels sports utiliser *jouer à* et *faire de*? Complétez la grille. *Can you remember which sports take* jouer à *and which take* faire de*? Fill in the grid.*

le tennis	J		l'athlétisme	
le ski	F		la pêche	
la voile			le basket	
la natation			le hockey	
l'équitation			les arts martiaux	
les boules			l'alpinisme	
le rugby				

Objectifs

- I can use the correct verb with each sport

 Ex. 5.15 Les jeunes français et le sport

Lisez l'infographie et répondez aux questions dans votre cahier. *Read the infographic and answer the questions in your copybook.*

1. What is the most popular sporting event for young people in France?

2. What is the least popular?

3. What would your order of preference be?

Les événements sportifs qui suscitent le plus d'intérêt pour les jeunes	
La Coupe du monde de football	54%
Les Jeux Olympiques	27%
Les tournois du Grand Chelem (R.Garros, Wimbledon etc.)	17%
La Ligue des Champions	13%
Le Super Bowl	9%
Le tournoi des Six Nations	5%
Le Tour de France	3%
Le Grand Prix de Monaco	2%

Objectifs

- I can read and understand a short infographic about sports in France

Ex. 5.16 Où est-ce que tu fais du sport ?

Les installations sportives

- le terrain de foot
- le terrain de tennis
- le terrain de golf
- le terrain de hockey

- le terrain de rugby
- le centre sportif
- la piscine
- la patinoire

- le centre équestre
- la mer
- le lac
- la montagne

Reliez les sports aux bons endroits pour les faire. *Match the sports with the correct locations.*

- le rugby
- la natation
- le tennis
- le foot

- le judo
- le patin à glace
- le golf
- le hockey

- la voile
- l'escalade
- le canoé

Visit **www.stadefrance.com** to learn more about the Stade de France.

- I can recognise and pronounce the vocabulary for sports venues

  # Ex. 5.17 Vocabulaire

Écoutez le CD et entrainez-vous à bien prononcer le vocabulaire. *Listen to the CD and repeat the vocabulary to improve your pronunciation.*

Quand est-ce que tu joues au foot ?

- Je joue au foot le …
- Quand est-ce que tu fais de la gymnastique ?
  Je fais de la gymnastique le …
- Je m'entraine …

- tous les lundis, mardis, mercredis …
- tous les jours, tous les soirs
- chaque weekend
- chaque soir

Unité 5 : Mon temps libre

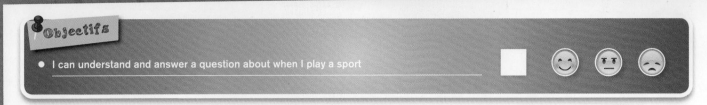

Objectifs

- I can understand and answer a question about when I play a sport

 Ex. 5.18 L'emploi du temps

Lisez l'emploi du temps du club d'activités et répondez aux questions dans votre cahier. *Read the sports timetable and answer the questions in your copybook.*

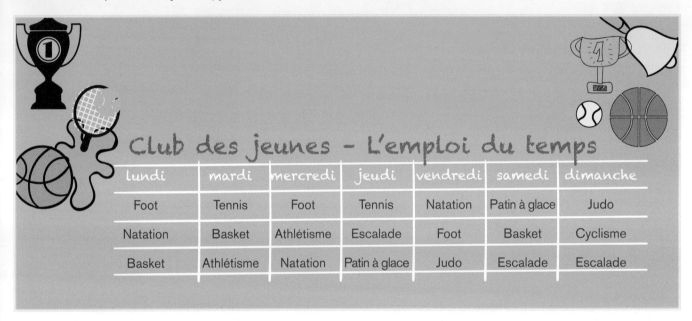

Club des jeunes – L'emploi du temps

lundi	mardi	mercredi	jeudi	vendredi	samedi	dimanche
Foot	Tennis	Foot	Tennis	Natation	Patin à glace	Judo
Natation	Basket	Athlétisme	Escalade	Foot	Basket	Cyclisme
Basket	Athlétisme	Natation	Patin à glace	Judo	Escalade	Escalade

1. On peut jouer au foot trois fois par semaine. Vrai ou faux ?

2. On peut faire de la natation trois fois par semaine. Vrai ou faux ?

3. On peut faire du patin à glace tous les jours. Vrai ou faux ?

4. On peut jouer au basket tous les lundis, mardis et samedis. Vrai ou faux ?

5. On peut faire de l'escalade tous les jeudis, vendredis et samedis. Vrai ou faux ?

6. On peut faire de l'athlétisme quatre fois par semaine. Vrai ou faux ?

7. On peut faire du judo chaque weekend ? Vrai ou faux ?

Objectifs

- I can read a simple sports timetable in French

142

Ex. 5.19

Écoutez les jeunes qui parlent de leur weekend et complétez la grille. *Listen to three young people talking about their weekends. Fill in the grid.*

	Matéo	Sébastien	Charlotte
Which sport?			
When?			
Where?			

Objectifs

● I can understand people talking about their weekend sports activities

 **Ex. 5.20 À deux**

À deux : posez les questions sur le sport à un(e) camarade et répondez à ses questions. Complétez la grille. *Talk with your partner about sports. Answer your partner's questions. Write your partner's answers in the grid below.*

Questions	Mes réponses	Les réponses de ma/mon camarade
Tu aimes le sport ?	Oui, j'aime … Non je n'aime pas …	
Tu fais quels sports ?	Je joue à la/au/aux … Je fais de la/du/des …	
Quand est-ce que tu joues à …/ fais de …		
Où est-ce que tu joues à …/fais de …		

Ex. 5.21 Interévaluation

First, fill in the grid below for yourself, then work with a partner to provide each other with feedback on your performances in Ex. 5.20.

Words I knew really well	
Words I didn't know	
Words I need to pronounce better	
Words I pronounced really well	
My intonation	

Depuis

Depuis means *since* or *for*.

● *Je joue au foot depuis sept ans.*
I've been playing football for seven years.

● *Je joue au foot depuis l'âge de 5 ans.*
I've been playing football since the age of 5.

In English, we use this sentence in the past tense.
In French, we use it in the present tense.

Ex. 5.22 Vocabulaire

Écoutez le CD et entraînez-vous à bien prononcer le vocabulaire. *Listen to the CD and repeat the vocabulary to improve your pronunciation.*

 Depuis quand est-ce que tu fais de la gymnastique ?

- Je fais de la gymnastique …
- depuis un an
- depuis deux ans
- depuis trois ans
- depuis l'âge de …
- depuis toujours !

Objectifs

- I can answer a question using the word *depuis* in my answer

  ## Ex. 5.23 Le blog d'Enzo

Lisez le blog d'Enzo et répondez aux questions dans votre cahier. *Read Enzo's blog and answer the questions in your copybook.*

(a) **Écoutez le CD et remplissez les blancs.** *Listen to the CD and fill in the blanks.*

(b) **Répondez aux questions dans votre cahier.** *Answer the questions in your copybook.*

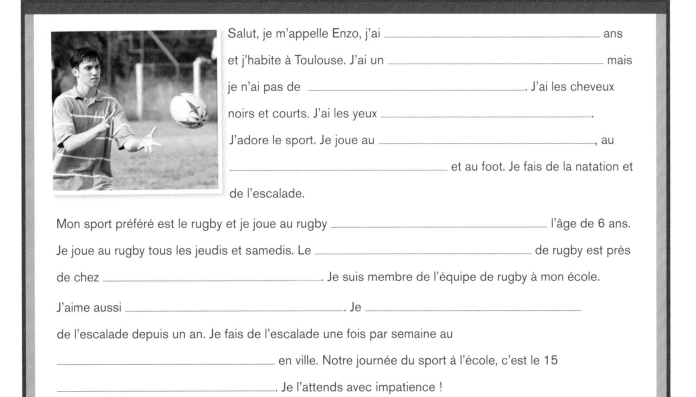

Salut, je m'appelle Enzo, j'ai _____ ans et j'habite à Toulouse. J'ai un _____ mais je n'ai pas de _____. J'ai les cheveux noirs et courts. J'ai les yeux _____. J'adore le sport. Je joue au _____, au _____ et au foot. Je fais de la natation et de l'escalade.

Mon sport préféré est le rugby et je joue au rugby _____ l'âge de 6 ans. Je joue au rugby tous les jeudis et samedis. Le _____ de rugby est près de chez _____. Je suis membre de l'équipe de rugby à mon école.

J'aime aussi _____. Je _____ de l'escalade depuis un an. Je fais de l'escalade une fois par semaine au _____ en ville. Notre journée du sport á l'école, c'est le 15 _____. Je l'attends avec impatience !

1. Enzo is 14 years old. True or false?
2. He lives in Toulouse. True or false?
3. He has two brothers. True or false?
4. Enzo has black hair and brown eyes. True or false?
5. What sports does he do?
6. What is his favourite sport?
7. How long has he been doing it?
8. When does he play it?
9. Is he a member of any teams?
10. Where does he go climbing?
11. What is happening on 15th September?

12. Find:
    (a) An example of the indefinite article – feminine
    (b) An example of a definite article – masculine
    (c) An –er verb in the present tense.

13. Translate:

near my house	
team	
once a week	
I can't wait for	

Objectifs

- I can read and understand a blog about a person's sports interests

Mon portfolio 5.1 : Le blog de mes sports préférés

Faites cet exercice dans votre portfolio. *Do this exercise in your portfolio.*

Ex. 5.24

Lisez le passage et répondez aux questions dans votre cahier. *Read the text and answer the questions in your copybook.*

Pour la 10ème édition de la Journée du sport scolaire, le CREPS de Boulouris, l'UNSS et l'Académie de Nice accueillent les 600 élèves des collèges du district Fréjus/Saint-Raphaël, le mercredi 14 septembre de 13h30 à 17h.

L'enjeu de cette journée nationale du sport scolaire est de promouvoir les activités des associations et des fédérations sportives scolaires teuprès des élèves, des équipes éducatives, des parents d'élèves et du monde sportif local.

Ce grand rendez-vous national donnera l'occasion à des milliers d'élèves de pratiquer et de découvrir de nombreuses activités sportives telles que : basket-ball, volley-ball, hand-ball, football, rugby, athlétisme, tennis de table, badminton et course d'orientation. Nul doute qu'il y a de la graine de champions parmi les élèves !

De plus, cette année, la Journée du sport scolaire s'intègre à l'opération « Sentez-vous sport » , avec pour marraine et parrain Laure Manaudou et Tony Parker.

CREPS de Boulouris
346, boulevard des Mimosas
83707 Saint-Raphaël

1. When is this sports day taking place?

2. What time does it begin?

3. It is for all students in the Fréjus/Saint-Raphaël district. True or false?

4. Name three sports offered in the area.

5. Why, do you think, are the two famous French sports personalities – Laure Manaudou and Tony Parker – mentioned here?

Objectifs

● I can read and understand the general message in an article about a sports day

 Ex. 5.25 La journée des sports

Lisez les tweets sur la journée des sports à l'école. Répondez aux questions en classe. *Read the tweets about school sports days. Answer the questions with your class.*

Amusez-vous bien au lycée St Michael, faites du sport!

Tweet 1

Journée du sport au collège Jules Vernes, samedi le 9 avril

Tweet 2

Journée du sport extraordinaire au collège Marie-Curie

Tweet 3

À vos marques, prêt, partez ! Journée du sport au collège Matisse

Tweet 4

1. Which tweet is about a sports day on a Saturday?

2. Which tweet says 'Ready, steady, go'?

3. How is the sports day described in *Collège Marie Curie*?

4. What does *Lycée St Michael* tell everyone to do?

Objectifs

● I can read and understand simple tweets about France's national school sports days

147

Ex. 5.26 Un tweet

Écrivez un tweet dans votre cahier pour promouvoir la journée des sports dans votre école. *Write a tweet in French in your copybook to promote the sports day in your school.*

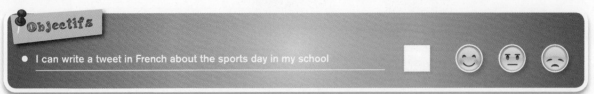

Objectifs

● I can write a tweet in French about the sports day in my school

  ## Ex. 5.27 Vocabulaire

Écoutez le CD et entrainez-vous à bien prononcer le vocabulaire. Puis, reliez les images aux bons mots-clés. *Listen to the CD and repeat the vocabulary to improve your pronunciation. Then match each image with one of the keywords.*

 Les passetemps

- la danse
- la télé
- la lecture
- la musique
- surfer sur Internet
- jouer aux jeux vidéo
- faire la cuisine

- le cinéma
- Je fais plein de choses !
- Je ne fais pas grand chose.
- Je mets à jour mon statut Facebook.

Objectifs

- I can recognise and understand the key words for pastimes 😊 😐 ☹️

  Ex. 5.28

Des jeunes parlent de leur weekend. *Listen to three young people talking about their weekends. Fill in the table.*

	Nathan	Inès	Clara
Which activity?			
When?			

Objectifs

- I can understand short conversations about what people like to do at the weekend 😊 😐 ☹️

 Ex. 5.29

Lisez les textes et répondez aux questions dans votre cahier. *Read the texts and answer the questions in your copybook.*

Jade

Moi, j'adore la musique. J'écoute de la musique sur mon iPod tous les jours. C'est cool. J'aime aussi la lecture et je lis chaque jour. Ça me détend.

Arthur

J'adore le cinéma. Je vais au cinéma chaque weekend. J'aime aussi surfer sur Internet parce que je chatte en ligne avec mes amis. C'est amusant, mes amis sont drôles.

Lucie

J'aime bien faire la cuisine, surtout faire des gâteaux parce que j'adore les gâteaux ! C'est trop bon ! Je fais la cuisine tous les samedis. J'adore aussi faire de la danse et je fais de la danse depuis l'âge de 5 ans. La danse, ça donne de l'énergie !

1. When does Jade listen to her iPod?
2. What does she also like, besides music?
3. When does Arthur go to the cinema?
4. Why does Arthur like surfing the net?
5. Why does Lucie like baking?
6. When does she bake?
7. How long has she been dancing?

8. Translate:

It's great	
It's relaxing	
It's delicious	
It's energising	
It's amusing/entertaining	

  ## Ex. 5.30 Le blog vidéo de Mathis

Regardez et écoutez la vidéo, puis répondez aux questions dans votre cahier.
Watch the video and answer the questions in your copybook.

1. Where does Mathis live?
2. How old is he?
3. What are his hobbies?
4. What does he do on Tuesday evenings?
5. Name one thing he likes to do at the weekend.
6. Next weekend, Mathis is visiting his cousin. True or false?

- I can read and understand short descriptions about how people like to spend their free time

 Les verbes en –ir   *–ir verbs*

Regular verbs that end in –ir are called *ir* verbs. To use an *–ir* verb in the present tense, you need to do the following:

1. Knock the –ir off the end of the verb: fin~~ir~~
2. Now you have the stem: fin–
3. Add the correct ending for the subject pronoun, as shown in the table below.

Subject pronouns	Stem	Endings	to finish
Je	fin	**is**	I finish, I am finishing
Tu	fin	**is**	You finish, You are finishing
Il	fin	**it**	He/it finishes, He/it is finishing

Elle	fin	**it**	She/it finishes, She/it is finishing
On	fin	**it**	One finishes/We finish, One is/We are finishing
Nous	fin	**issons**	We finish, We are finishing
Vous	fin	**issez**	You finish, You are finishing
Ils	fin	**issent**	They finish, They are finishing
Elles	fin	**issent**	They finish, They are finishing

  Ex. 5.31 Le verbe *finir*

Écoutez le CD et répétez le verbe *finir*. *Listen to the CD and repeat the verb finir.*

Objectifs
● I can recognise and understand the verb *finir* in the present tense

Astuces

Can you remember the difference between regular and irregular verbs? We have already learned that, in French, there are three families of regular verbs: –er, –ir and –re. We learned about –er verbs in Unité 4. Now we have learned about – ir verbs. Study and remember the verb endings for the regular –ir verb *finir*. Then you can use those endings for all regular –ir verbs.

Objectifs
● I can understand and explain about –ir and –er verbs in the present tense

 Ex. 5.32

With your partner, think about –ir verbs. How do we form an –ir verb in the present tense? *What are the verb endings? Take turns in explaining and describing –ir verbs to each other.*

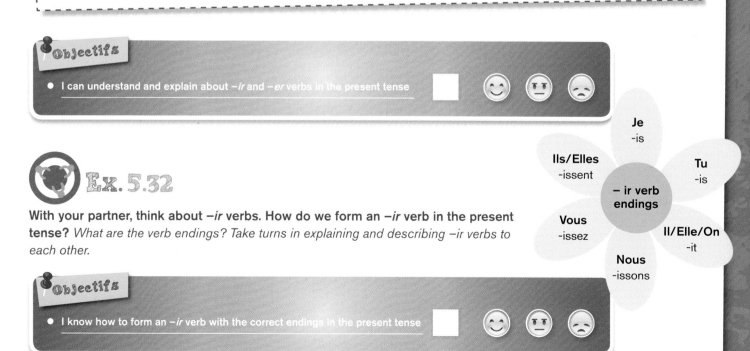

Objectifs
● I know how to form an –ir verb with the correct endings in the present tense

151

Astuces

When we list a verb (e.g. *je finis, tu finis,* and so on), we call this conjugating a verb. We are making sure that we have the right verb endings for each subject pronoun.

Ex. 5.33 Les verbes en -ir

Conjuguez les verbes en –ir. *Conjugate these –ir verbs.*

Remplir *(to fill in)*	Grandir *(to grow up)*	Rougir *(to blush)*
Je		
Tu		
Il/elle		
On		
Nous		
Vous		
Ils/elles		

Ex. 5.34

Reliez chacun des verbes en –ir ci-dessous avec sa traduction en anglais. *Match these –ir verbs. Write the verb and its meaning in your copybook.*

rougir	to think, to reflect
vieillir	to fill in
réfléchir	to catch, to seize
saisir	to build
grandir	to blush
obéir	to grow up, to get bigger
bâtir	to obey
choisir	to grow old
remplir	to choose

Astuces

As you learn French, keep looking for cognates that will help you to work out the meanings of new words. With your partner, discuss the cognates in Ex. 5.34. How did you work out the meaning of each verb?

Ex. 5.35

Complétez les phrases avec la bonne forme du verbe entre parenthèses. *Fill in the blanks using the correct verb ending.*

1. Tu _____ (remplir) le sac.

2. Ils _____ (saisir) le ballon.

3. Elles _____ (rougir) quelquefois.

4. Nous _____ (obéir) à nos parents.

5. Tu _____ (bâtir) un grand mur.

6. Il _____ (grandir).

7. Elle _____ (réfléchir) beaucoup.

8. Je _____ (choisir) le pull bleu.

Objectifs

- I understand and can use –*ir* verbs in sentences

- I can conjugate –*ir verbs*

Ex. 5.36 À mon avis ...

Work with your partner to revise the vocabulary we learned for the Group Talk in Unité 1.

- J'aime. ♥
- J'adore. ♥♥
- Je n'aime pas. ✗
- Je déteste. ✗✗
- Oui, moi aussi.

- Je suis d'accord.
- Tu as tort.
- Tu as raison.
- Tu rigoles.
- Tu es fou.

- Tu es folle.
- C'est cool.
- C'est super cool !
- Moi, mon truc, c'est ...
- Ce n'est pas mon truc.

Ex. 5.37 Group Talk

You are going to use the images below for your Group Talk, so you need to ensure that you know what they are in French. You must decide which you like, dislike, love or hate!

1. _____

2. _____

3. _____

 4. _____

5. _____

6. _____

 Votre discussion de groupe. *Your Group Talk.*
Group Talk Step 1

J'aime	J'adore	Je n'aime pas	Je déteste

Group Talk Step 2

Lisez votre liste à voix haute à un(e) camarade. *Read your list out loud with your partner to practise your pronunciation.*

Group Talk Step 3

Now you're ready to do your own Group Talk. You can do this either in pairs or in small groups like those you saw in the Group Talk video in Unité 1. You have already looked at the images and you have already decided which you like, love, dislike or hate.

- Remember to use the images and the Group Talk phrases to give your opinion.
- The first person starts by giving their opinion on one of the images. Moving around the table, each student can either agree or disagree. When you get more confident, you can jump into the conversation at any point and disagree or agree with the other students in the group! It's often fun to have one student who is secretly chosen to always disagree. They can cause a lot of drama during the Group Talk!

Objectifs

- I can pronounce all of the *mots-clés* with a French accent
- I can participate in a Group Talk

Un verbe irrégulier : Aller – *to go*

Aller is a verb that you have met many times before: it was one of the first verbs you learned. Do you remember this question: *Ça va?*

We translate that as 'How are you?' but a literal translation is 'How is it going?'

Aller is a very useful verb – one you will use a lot – so make sure you learn it off by heart.

aller	to go
Je vais	I go, I am going
Tu vas	You go, You are going
Il va	He/it goes, He/it is going
Elle va	She/it goes, She/it is going
On va	One goes/We go, One is going/We are going
Nous allons	We go, We are going
Vous allez	You go, You are going
Ils vont	They go, They are going
Elles vont	They go, They are going

155

Search YouTube for *'the verb aller-to go by Étienne'*. Which of your classmates can rap the verb *aller* to the best beat?

 Ex. 5.38 À deux

Répondez aux questions avec un(e) camarade.
With your partner, answer these questions.

- Why does the preposition *à* change?

- What other verb uses the preposition *à*?

- Explain the grammar rules for the preposition *à*.

Objectifs

- I can recognise and conjugate the irregular verb *aller*
- I can understand and use the preposition *à* with the verb *aller*

 Ex. 5.39 Le Verbe *aller*

Complétez les phrases avec la bonne forme du verbe *aller*. *Fill in the blanks using the correct form of the verb* aller.

1. Je _____ au cinéma parce que j'aime voir des films.

2. Nous _____ au terrain de foot parce que nous aimons jouer au foot.

3. Ils _____ à la piscine parce qu'ils aiment la natation.

4. Elle _____ au centre sportif parce qu'elle aime le sport.

5. Tu _____ au terrain de golf parce que tu aimes le golf.

 Ex. 5.40

Complétez les phrases avec la bonne forme du verbe *aller* et de la préposition à (au, à la, à l'). *Fill in the blanks using the correct form of the verb* aller *and the correct form of the preposition:* au, à la *or* à l'.

1. Nous _____ _____ piscine parce que nous aimons la natation.

2. Ils _____ _____ cinéma avec leurs amis.

3. Elle _____ _____ terrain de foot pour faire un match de foot.

4. On _____ _____ centre sportif pour faire de l'athlétisme.

5. Vous _____ _____ centre équestre parce que vous aimez l'équitation.

  ## Ex. 5.41 Les saisons

Écoutez le CD et entrainez-vous à bien prononcer le vocabulaire. *Listen to the CD and repeat the vocabulary to improve your pronunciation.*

Les saisons

- le printemps
- l'été
- l'automne
- l'hiver

 We say **en** été for in summer, **en** automne for in autumn and **en** hiver for in winter.

But we say **au** printemps for in spring.

Objectifs

- **I can say the names of the seasons in French**

Ex. 5.42 Le temps

Écoutez le CD et entraînez-vous à bien prononcer le vocabulaire. Puis, reliez les images aux bons mots-clés.
Listen to the CD and repeat the vocabulary to improve your pronunciation. Then match each image with a keyword.

Quel temps fait-il ?

1. Il fait beau.
2. Il fait mauvais.
3. Il fait froid.
4. Il fait chaud.
5. Il y a des nuages.

6. Il y a du soleil.
7. Il y a du vent.
8. Il pleut.
9. Il gèle.
10. Il neige.

Objectifs

- I can recognise and understand keywords for weather

Astuces

Le temps means 'the weather' but *la météo* means 'the weather forecast'.

Idioms are phrases that have a figurative meaning rather than a literal one. For example, in English we might say 'The car caught my eye', meaning that we noticed the car. There are many interesting French idioms. What do you think the idioms below mean? Are there any idioms in English that mean something similar?

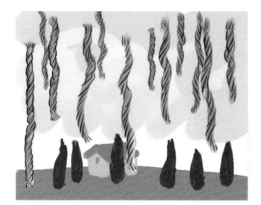

Il pleut des cordes !

Il fait un temps de chien !

Objectifs

● I can pronounce and understand weather vocabulary

Ex. 5.43 La météo

Écoutez la météo et répondez aux questions. Cochez la bonne réponse : (a), (b) ou (c). Réécoutez et vérifiez.

Listen to the weather reports and choose the correct description. Listen again and check your answers.

1. Dans l'ouest …
   (a) il y a du soleil.
   (b) il fait mauvais.
   (c) il fait froid.

2. Dans le sud …
   (a) il fait chaud .
   (b) il fait beau.
   (c) il neige.

3. Dans le nord …
   (a) il y a du vent.
   (b) il fait chaud.
   (c) il gèle.

4. Dans l'est …
   (a) il fait froid.
   (b) il pleut.
   (c) il gèle.

Objectifs

● I can understand a simple weather forecast in French

Ex. 5.44 Les loisirs et le temps

Regardez les images et décrivez vos activités. *Look at the images and describe what you do in each type of weather.*

Qu'est-ce que tu fais quand il fait beau ?	
Qu'est-ce que tu fais quand il fait froid ?	
Qu'est-ce que tu fais quand il pleut ?	
Qu'est-ce que tu fais quand il y a du soleil ?	
Qu'est-ce que tu fais tu quand il gèle ?	

Objectifs

- I know French vocabulary for the weather off by heart
- I can say which activities I do in different weathers

Mon portfolio 5.2 : La météo

Faites cet exercice dans votre portfolio. *Do this exercise in your portfolio.*

Ex. 5.45 La lettre de Fabien

Lisez la lettre de Fabien et répondez aux questions. *Read Fabien's letter and answer the questions.*

Lille, le 14 novembre

Cher James,

Salut ! Moi, je m'appelle Fabien et j'ai 14 ans. J'habite à Lille près de la frontière belge. J'ai les yeux verts et les cheveux blonds et bouclés. J'habite dans un appartement au centre-ville. Il y a quatre chambres, un salon, une cuisine, une salle à manger et un bureau. Il y a trois salles de bains et une buanderie. J'aime notre appartement parce qu'il est confortable et on a tout sur place dans le quartier. Parle-moi de ta maison.

J'ai un frère et une sœur. Je suis l'aîné. Ma sœur Laetitia a 9 ans et mon frère Stéphane a 11 ans. Tu as des frères et sœurs ? Laetitia est bavarde et drôle. Elle adore la musique, le foot et regarder la télé avec ses amis. Stéphane est sociable et intelligent. Il aime l'athlétisme et le hockey. Il joue au hockey avec son équipe au terrain de hockey, près de chez nous. Tu aimes le sport ?

Je suis sportif aussi : je joue au foot, au rugby et je fais de la natation. Il y a une piscine près de chez nous et un centre sportif aussi. Je joue au foot et au rugby depuis l'âge de 7 ans. Je fais de la natation depuis 5 ans. Pendant l'été, quand il fait beau, je joue au foot avec mes amis. C'est cool et je m'amuse bien. Pendant l'hiver, quand il fait froid, je joue au rugby et je fais du ski. C'est super, le ski ! Ça donne de l'énergie et j'adore la neige ! Quand il pleut, j'aime bien aller à la piscine et j'aime aussi aller au cinéma avec mes amis. Nous choisissons des films d'aventure. Quels sont tes passetemps ?

Je vais au collège à Lille. Je suis en sixième. Mon collège est très grand et il y a un centre sportif et une piscine aussi. Tu es en quelle année ? Tu aimes ton école ?

Je dois te quitter maintenant.

Écris-moi vite!

À bientôt,

Fabien

1. Where is Lille located?

2. Describe Fabien.

3. Why does Fabien like his family's apartment?

4. Who is the eldest in his family?

5. Describe Laetitia.

6. What are Stéphane's hobbies?

7. What sport does Fabien play in summer when the weather is nice?

8. Which sports does he play in winter when it is cold?

9. What does he do when it is raining?

10. What films do Fabien and his friends choose?

11. Where does he go to school?

12. What year is he in?

13. Find:

    (a) an example of the verb *aller*

    (b) an adjective

    (c) an –*ir* verb.

14. Translate:

We have everything on our doorstep.	
It's great, and I enjoy myself.	
It's energising.	
I have to go now.	

Objectifs

- I can read and understand a letter about hobbies and free time

Mon portfolio 5.3 : Une lettre pour décrire mes passetemps

Faites cet exercice dans votre portfolio. *Do this exercise in your portfolio.*

Récapitulatif

Mots-clés pour l'Unité 5

Les sports

- le foot
- le tennis
- le basket

- le rugby
- le ping-pong
- le golf

- la pétanque/les boules
- le hockey

Des sports individuels

- le cyclisme
- l'alpinisme
- l'escalade
- la planche à voile
- la natation
- le patin à glace

- le patinage
- l'athlétisme
- l'équitation
- le ski
- le ski nautique
- le canoë

- la pêche
- la plongée
- la voile
- le judo
- la course à pied

Les installations sportives

- le terrain de foot
- le terrain de tennis
- le terrain de golf
- le terrain de hockey

- le terrain de rugby
- le centre sportif
- la piscine
- la patinoire

- le centre équestre
- la mer
- le lac
- la montagne

Quand est-ce que tu joues au foot ?

- Je joue au foot le …

- Quand est-ce que tu fais de la gymnastique ?
  Je fais la gymnastique le …

- Je m'entraine …

- tous les lundis, mardis, mercredis …
- tous les jours, tous les soirs
- chaque weekend
- chaque soir

Depuis quand est-ce que tu fais de la gymnastique ?

- Je fais de la gymnastique …
- depuis un an
- depuis deux ans

- depuis trois ans
- depuis l'âge de …
- depuis toujours !

Les passetemps

- la danse
- la télé
- la lecture
- la musique
- surfer sur Internet
- jouer aux jeux vidéo
- faire la cuisine
- le cinéma
- Je fais plein de choses !
- Je ne fais pas grand chose.
- Je mets à jour mon statut Facebook.

Les saisons

- le printemps
- l'été
- l'automne
- l'hiver

Quel temps fait-il ?

- Il fait beau.
- Il fait mauvais.
- Il fait froid.
- Il fait chaud.
- Il y a des nuages.
- Il y a du soleil.
- Il y a du vent.
- Il pleut.
- Il gèle.
- Il neige.

Bilan de l'Unité 5. *Checklist for Unit 5.*

Pour chaque objectif, choisissez votre émoticône.	😊	😐	😞
Listening			
I can understand people telling me what sports they play or do			
I can understand people telling me what their favourite sport is			
I can understand people saying when, where and for how long they've been playing a sport			
I can understand people telling me what their hobbies are			
I can understand a short, simple weather forecast			
I can understand people telling me how they spend their free time, based on the weather			
I can understand people giving their opinion about their hobbies and sports in a group.			
Reading			
I can read a short blog about hobbies and sports			
I can read an infographic about French people's tastes in sport			
I can read a simple description about favourite hobbies and sports			
I can read a short letter about hobbies and sports			
I can read a tweet about a sports day			
I can read a timetable for a sports centre			
Spoken production			
I can say what sports I play and why			
I can say when, where and for how long I've been playing a sport			
I can say what my hobbies are			
I can say what I do in my free time, depending on the weather			
I can describe the weather in a short sentence, and give a simple weather forecast			

Unité 5 : Mon temps libre

Spoken interaction			
I can ask my friend about the sports they play and why			
I can ask my friend about when, where and for how long they have been playing a sport			
I can ask about the weather and what someone does depending on the weather			
I can give my opinion in a group about my hobbies and sports			
I can agree or disagree with someone's opinion, using a short sentence			
Writing			
I can write short answers to questions about my favourite sport			
I can write a short blog about the sports I play: when, where, how often and for how long			
I can write a letter to my pen pal about my hobbies and sports			
I can write a tweet about my school's sports day			
I can write a short weather forecast			

Discutez en classe. Have a class discussion.

- Look back over your Portfolio exercises. In which areas did you give yourself stars?
- Look at your wishes. Have any of these improved?
- What was your favourite part of Unité 5? Why?
- What did you least enjoy in Unité 5? Why?
- Have you found any new ways to help you learn French?
- Think about the next unit you will work on. What are you looking forward to learning more about? Why?

UNITÉ 6

À table

By the end of this unit you will

- Say what you like to eat at mealtimes
- Hear and understand a video blog about meals
- Hear and understand a shopping list
- Play fun French-speaking games about food
- Ask and answer questions about mealtimes
- Give your opinion about food
- Read and write a school lunch menu
- Make an order in an ice cream parlour
- Read and understand a short letter about French meals and foods
- Count from 1 to 100
- Hear and say phone numbers in French
- Read and understand a short French recipe
- Read and write a blog about meals

 ## Ex. 6.1 La Vie en France

Regardez la vidéo et répondez aux questions. *Watch the video and answer the questions.*

1. What does *cordon bleu* mean?

2. Name one place where there is a *cordon bleu* school.

3. What language is spoken during teaching at a *cordon bleu* school?

4. What must students do to pass their exam at the end of their *cordon bleu* course?

5. How can French students and their parents find out the school lunch menu?

6. Give an example of a starter, a main course and a dessert for a typical lunch in France.

7. Name one of the famous cheeses mentioned in this clip.

8. Name one rule on school lunches set by the Minister for Education in France.

9. Name a popular *gouter* for children.

10. What is an *apéritif*?

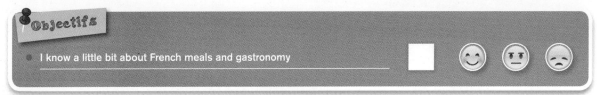

Objectifs

- I know a little bit about French meals and gastronomy

 ## Ex. 6.2 Sondage en classe

1. What are the favourite dinners in your class?

2. How many of these dishes are French?

- Go to **www.cordonbleu.edu** to learn about culinary school and gastronomy.

- Research Michelin Stars and how they are awarded.

- Visit **http://restaurantgeorgesparis.com/fr/** to see a cool restaurant on the top floor of the Georges Pompidou Centre in Paris.

  ## Ex. 6.3 Le petit déjeuner

Écoutez le CD et entrainez-vous à bien prononcer le vocabulaire. Puis, reliez les images avec les bons mots-clés.
Listen to the CD and repeat the vocabulary to improve your pronunciation. Then match each image with a keyword.

Le petit déjeuner

- le café
- le thé
- le lait
- le jus d'orange
- le sucre

- le chocolat chaud
- un croissant
- le pain grillé
- une tartine
- le pain

- la confiture
- le beurre
- les céréales

 **Ex. 6.4**

Dans votre cahier, faites la liste de ce que vous mangez le matin au petit déjeuner. Utilisez votre dictionnaire si besoin est. *In your copybook, write a list of what you usually eat for breakfast. Use a dictionary to find the vocabulary you need.*

Objectifs

- I know the keywords for breakfast

Ex. 6.5 Le déjeuner

Écoutez le CD et entrainez-vous à bien prononcer le vocabulaire. Puis, reliez les images avec les bons mots-clés.
Listen to the CD and repeat the vocabulary to improve your pronunciation. Then match each image with a keyword.

Le déjeuner

- une crêpe
- un sandwich
- le jambon
- une salade
- l'huile d'olive
- les œufs
- la soupe
- un croque-monsieur
- un croque-madame
- l'eau

 # Ex. 6.6

(a) **Dans votre cahier, faites la liste de ce que vous mangez le midi, au déjeuner. Utilisez votre dictionnaire si besoin est.** *In your copybook, write a list of what you usually eat for lunch. Use a dictionary to find the vocabulary you need.*

(b) **Les jeunes décrivent ce qu'ils mangent aux deux repas. Complétez la grille.** *The teenagers describe what they have at mealtimes. Write the information into the correct column.*

	Breakfast	Lunch
Léa		
Emma		
Josh		

Objectifs

- I know the keywords for lunch

Ex. 6.7 Le diner

Écoutez le CD et entrainez-vous à bien prononcer le vocabulaire. *Listen to the CD and repeat the vocabulary to improve your pronunciation.*

Le diner

- le poulet
- le bœuf
- le poisson
- des légumes
- du riz
- des pâtes
- des frites

  Ex. 6.8 Les desserts

(a) **Écoutez le CD et entrainez-vous à bien prononcer le vocabulaire.** *Listen to the CD and repeat the vocabulary to improve your pronunciation.*

Le dessert

- la tarte aux pommes
- le gâteau
- la glace
- une crêpe
- un yaourt
- un fruit
- le fromage

 (b) **Les jeunes décrivent ce qu'ils mangent aux trois repas. Complétez la bonne colonne.**
The teenagers describe what they have at mealtimes. Write the information into the correct column.

	Breakfast	Lunch	Dinner
Simon			
Julie			
Amélie			

Ex. 6.9

Dans votre cahier, faites la liste de ce que vous mangez le soir, au diner, et aussi ce que vous mangez comme dessert. Utilisez votre dictionnaire si besoin est. *In your copybook, write a list of what you usually eat for dinner and dessert. Use a dictionary to find the vocabulary you need.*

Make vocabulary flash cards so that you can learn and remember the keywords for food and mealtimes. Websites such as **www.studystacks.com** are useful for this.

   Ex. 6.10 Les quantités

(a)   Écoutez le CD et entrainez-vous à bien prononcer le vocabulaire. *Listen to the CD and repeat the vocabulary to improve your pronunciation.*

Les quantités

- une tranche de ...
- un morceau de ...
- un litre de ...
- une tasse de ...
- un verre de

(b)   Les jeunes décrivent ce qu'ils mangent et en quelles quantités. Complétez la grille. *The teenagers describe what they eat and in what portions. Write the information into the correct column.*

	Nourriture	Quantité
Jules	jambon	2 tranches
Benjamin		
Louise		
Marie		

- I know the keywords for quantities of foods

 **Ex. 6.11**

Traduisez le nom des aliments et cherchez-les dans la grille de mots cachés. *Translate the names of these foods and find them in the word search.*

Anglais	Français
vegetables	
cheese	
chicken	
chips	
jam	

Anglais	Français
ham	
sugar	
fish	
lunch	
slice	

T	R	A	N	C	H	E	P	C	B	J	F	P	F	J
U	C	A	D	Y	I	I	O	O	A	N	R	H	E	G
Q	Q	I	N	W	F	N	D	M	U	Y	I	F	I	P
J	Z	J	T	J	F	S	B	U	T	L	T	H	U	T
N	H	C	X	I	U	O	E	K	H	A	E	T	C	U
H	V	F	T	S	N	Y	Y	M	X	M	S	T	E	H
J	R	U	M	Q	J	Q	D	I	U	M	C	N	G	G
Q	R	E	N	U	E	J	E	D	Z	G	O	O	A	H
E	N	J	N	L	F	G	B	I	E	S	E	R	M	G
P	F	J	B	D	D	H	J	A	S	G	V	L	O	J
M	M	O	E	E	K	Z	M	I	R	W	Z	V	R	G
P	P	U	Y	D	N	Q	O	E	R	C	U	S	F	R
C	E	F	Y	S	K	P	U	N	F	M	S	J	F	G
R	B	N	H	U	G	W	W	L	I	M	O	W	Q	B
Q	O	N	A	D	A	A	W	Y	E	N	X	E	G	W

Le verbe manger *to eat*

At first glance, the verb *manger* looks like a regular –*er* verb and it pretty much is, apart from one small spelling change. Can you spot this in Ex. 6.12?

  # Ex. 6.12 Le verbe manger

Écoutez le CD et répétez le verbe *manger*. *Listen to the CD and repeat the verb* manger.

manger	to eat		On mange	One eats/We eat, One is eating/We are eating
Je mange	I eat, I am eating		Nous mangeons	We eat, We are eating
Tu manges	You eat, You are eating		Vous mangez	You eat, You are eating
Il mange	He/it eats, He/it is eating		Ils mangent	They eat, They are eating
Elle mange	She/it eats, She/it is eating		Elles mangent	They eat, They are eating

 # Ex. 6.13

With your partner, think about the differences between regular and irregular verbs. *What happens with the verb stems and verb endings? Take turns in explaining and describing this to each other.*

  # Ex. 6.14 Le verbe *boire*

Écoutez le CD et répétez le verbe *boire*. *Listen to the CD and repeat the verb* boire.

boire	to drink		On boit	One drinks/We drink, One is drinking /We are drinking
Je bois	I drink, I am drinking		Nous buvons	We drink, We are drinking
Tu bois	You drink, You are drinking		Vous buvez	You drink, You are drinking
Il boit	He/it drinks, He/it is drinking		Ils boivent	They drink, They are drinking
Elle boit	She/it drinks, She/it is drinking		Elles boivent	They drink, They are drinking

Le verbe *boire* *to drink*

It is clear when we look at the verb *boire* that it is irregular. However, to remember our verbs, even the irregular ones, it is helpful to try to find any type of pattern. What pattern can you find for the stem or endings in the verb *boire*?

Astuces
Tips for remembering verbs

- **Flash cards:** The more you use a verb, the more you will remember it. Create flash cards with the subject pronouns on one set of cards and the matching part of the verb on another set. Use the flash cards to play games such as Snap or Go Fish. Try any game that might help you to visualise the verb, its spelling and its pronoun.

- **Music:** Search websites such as YouTube for verb videos and songs to help you learn irregular verbs.

- **Eagle Eye:** Language is very much about patterns, so try to develop an eagle eye for them! Even though an irregular verb doesn't have a strict pattern, there might be some common element in it that you can see and remember. Often the verb endings for *je* and *tu* are the same. Sometimes *nous* and *vous* have a different stem from the rest of the subject pronouns. Can you see an example of this in *boire* in Ex. 6.14?

- **Colour coding:** Write out verb conjugations and use a highlighter to show any patterns. This draws your eye to the key element and helps you to visualise the verb next time you use it.

It can be helpful to know what type of learner you are: some people are visual learners, some are auditory learners, some are kinestheic (active) learners, etc. Visit **http://www.whatismylearningstyle.com/learning-style-test-1.html** to find out about your learning style. Research online to find study tips that suit your style of learning.

Objectifs
- I can conjugate the irregular verbs *manger* and *boire*

Ex. 6.15

Complétez les phrases avec la bonne forme des verbes *manger* et *boire*. *Fill in the blanks using the correct part of the verbs* manger *or* boire.

1. Nous (manger) _____ du pain grillé.
2. Ils (boire) _____ du café au lait.
3. Je (boire) _____ de l'eau froide.
4. Vous (manger) _____ du poulet.
5. Ils (boire) _____ du jus d'orange.
6. Je (manger) _____ des croissants.

Ex. 6.16 Le blog vidéo de Camille

Regardez le blog vidéo de Camille. Elle parle de ses repas. *Watch the video of Camille. She is talking about her meals.*

1. At what time does Camille eat breakfast?

2. What does she have for breakfast?

3. At what time does she have lunch in the canteen?

4. Name one item on her school menu.

Objectifs

- I understand a video blog about meals ☐ 😊 😐 ☹

 L'article partitif *Partitive article*

We use *l'article partitif* when we want to say the words 'some' or 'any' in French.

The basic word for 'some' or 'any' is *de*. However, *de* changes its spelling depending on the gender of the noun and whether it is singular or plural.

de + le = **du** (m)	du fromage	=	some cheese
de + la = **de la** (f)	de la glace	=	some ice cream
de + plural = **des**	des croissants	=	some croissants
de + words beginning with a vowel = **de l'**	de l'eau	=	some water

 ## Ex. 6.17 L'article partitif

Complétez les phrases avec la bonne forme de l'article partitif. *Fill in the blanks with the correct form of l'article partitif.*

1. Je bois _____ (de la/du) thé.

2. Tu bois _____ (du/des) jus d'orange?

3. Ils mangent _____ (du/des) légumes.

4. Vous mangez _____ (du/de la) pain avec _____ (des/de la) confiture?

5. Nous buvons _____ (de l'/de la) eau.

6. Nous mangeons _____ (de la/du) riz.

7. Tu manges _____ (des/du) croissants?

8. Elle boit _____ (des/du) lait.

9. Ils boivent _____ (de l'/du) café.

10. Je mange _____ (des/du) pain grillé.

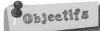

  ## Ex. 6.18 Au supermarché

Léa fait des courses au supermarché. Écoutez le CD et écrivez ce qui manque sur sa liste de courses. *Léa is shopping at the supermarket. Listen to the CD and write down the things that are missing from her shopping list.*

1. _____

2. _____

3. _____

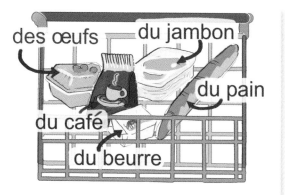

 ## Ex. 6.19 Je m'appelle Madame/ Monsieur Perrier ...

Écoutez votre professeur expliquer les règles du jeu. *Listen to your teacher, who will explain the rules of the game* Je m'appelle Madame/Monsieur Perrier.

Ex. 6.20 Quiz en classe

Work with your partner to create a 10-question class quiz on what you have learned so far in Unité 6. You could ask for French translations of new words, explanations of grammar points, conjugations of verbs, etc. Make sure that your quiz tests the things that you have learned in this unit so far!

Exemple :

1. The French word for 'lunch' is **(a)** *le petit déjeuner* **(b)** *le déjeuner* or **(c)** *la confiture*?

Astuces

The phrases 'I am hungry' and 'I am thirsty' are formed using the verb *avoir* – to have:

J'ai ***faim***   I'm hungry   J'ai ***soif***   I'm thirsty.

Think about any other languages you know. How can you say 'I am hungry' – do you use the verb 'to have'? Remember that languages do not always translate exactly: it is important to adapt a translation to get the correct version and meaning in English or French.

 Ex. 6.21 Je mange, je bois ...

Écoutez votre professeur expliquer les règles du jeu *Je mange, je bois*. *Listen to your teacher, who will explain the rules of the game* Je mange, je bois.

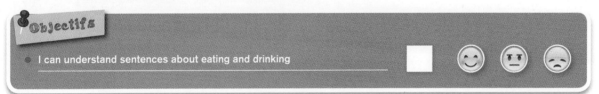

Objectifs

● I can understand sentences about eating and drinking

  Ex. 6.22

CD 2 T 29

Les jeunes décrivent ce qu'ils mangent aux trois repas. Complétez la grille. *The teenagers describe what they have at mealtimes. Write the information into the correct column.*

	Breakfast	Lunch	Dinner
Max			
Marie			
Lucas			
Sarah			

 **Ex. 6.23 À deux**

À deux: posez les questions sur les repas à votre camarade et répondez à ses questions. Complétez la grille. *Talk with your classmate. Ask them questions and reply to theirs. Fill in the grid with your answers and theirs.*

Questions	Mes réponses	Les réponses de ma/mon camarade
Qu'est-ce que tu manges le matin (au petit déjeuner) ?		
Qu'est-ce que tu manges le midi/au déjeuner ?		
Qu'est-ce que tu manges au gouter ?		
Qu'est-ce que tu manges le soir (au diner) ?		

Objectifs

- I can speak about my mealtimes, and ask my partner about their mealtimes

☺ 😐 ☹

Ex. 6.24 Interévaluation

First, fill in the grid below for yourself, then work with a partner to provide each other with feedback on your performances in Ex. 6.23.

Words I knew really well	
Words I didn't know	
Words I need to pronounce better	
Words I pronounced really well	
My intonation	

French students can have their lunch in their school canteen. Many schools post their menus online every week or every month so that students and parents know what will be on offer.

 ## Ex. 6.25 Le blog de Lucie

Lisez le texte et répondez aux questions. *Read the extract and answer the questions.*

Le matin, au petit déjeuner, je mange une tartine et je bois un jus d'orange. J'ai toujours faim le matin. En hiver, j'aime bien boire un chocolat chaud. Le midi, je déjeune au restaurant scolaire et là, le menu est très bien et très varié. Il y a de la viande, du poisson ou du poulet. Le menu est affiché en ligne. Mon plat préféré, c'est le poisson parce que je trouve ça très bon. J'adore le fromage aussi. Après le collège, j'aime bien prendre un gouter. En général, je mange un fruit et je bois du café. Le soir, je mange à la maison avec ma famille. J'aide mes parents à préparer le diner. J'aime bien faire la cuisine. En général, nous mangeons de la soupe, du poulet, des pâtes, du fromage et un fruit. J'adore le poulet rôti. Maman et Papa prennent un petit verre de vin et mon frère et moi, nous buvons de l'eau.

(a) Vrai ou faux ?

1. Le matin, au petit déjeuner, Lucie mange une tartine.
2. Elle n'a pas faim le matin.
3. En hiver, elle aime boire du café.
4. Le midi, elle déjeune au restaurant scolaire.
5. Le menu du restaurant scolaire est affiché en ligne.
6. Le menu n'est pas très varié.
7. Son plat préféré, c'est le bœuf.
8. Elle adore le fromage.
9. Elle mange un fruit après le collège.
10. Elle prépare le diner toute seule.

(b) Reliez les débuts et fins de phrases suivants.

Le matin, au petit déjeuner	au restaurant scolaire.
Après le collège,	avec ma famille.
Le midi, je déjeune	je mange une tartine.
Le soir, je mange à la maison	j'aime bien prendre un gouter.
Mon frère et moi, nous buvons	de l'eau.

(c) **Soulignez chaque article partitif + nom dans le texte ci-dessus. Complétez la grille.** *Underline the partitive article with its nouns in the passage. Write them into the correct column below.*

du	de la	des	de l'

Astuces

When we speak, we use small words as we think about our answers. In English, these filler words and sounds include 'well', 'eh' and 'so'. In French, we can use filler words and sounds such as *euh, bon, alors*, etc. Try to include these in your spoken French. They will give you an authentic, natural intonation as you speak. They will also give you time to think, as you consider your answer to a question!

Ex. 6.26 À mon avis ...

Regardez les images et donnez votre avis. *With your partner, look at the images and give your opinion. Use a dictionary to check the meanings of any phrases you don't know.*

- J'adore.
- J'aime.
- J'aime bien.
- Je n'aime pas.

- Je n'aime pas du tout.
- Je déteste.
- C'est super bon !
- C'est bon.

- Je trouve ça très bon.
- C'est dégoutant(e).

Objectifs

- I can give opinions about food

Ex. 6.27 La gastronomie

Regardez la vidéo et répondez aux questions. *Look at the video and answer the questions.*

1. What well-known French soup is described in this clip?

2. Name two ingredients in *salade niçoise*.

3. *Bœuf bourguignon* comes from which French region?

4. What festival occurs every August in Burgundy?

5. How did *tarte tatin* get its name?

6. What does the word 'soufflé' mean?

Objectifs

- I know about French food culture

Astuces

When we read a new text in French, we will always come across words we haven't met before. Rather than immediately reaching for the dictionary, try some of these strategies first.

- Read the title and see if any pictures alongside the text can help you to guess the topic.

- Pay attention to the words you **do** know. This is encouraging: you might be surprised at how much you know already.

- Look out for cognates (see p.4).

- Try reading the questions before you read the text passage: this can give you useful clues.

- Use a highlighter to identify a question and the passage of text that you think might contain the answer. Use different coloured highlighters for each question and relevant piece of text.

- Underline the words that you think will hold key information. If you don't understand these key words, find their meanings in the dictionary.

Ex. 6.28

Le menu d'un lycée de Lyon. Lisez le menu et répondez aux questions. *Here is a menu from a lycée in Lyon. Read the menu and answer the questions.*

Lundi	Mardi	Mercredi	Jeudi	Vendredi
****	****	****	****	****
Salade verte	Salade verte	Salade verte	Salade de lentilles	Salade verte
Taboulé à la menthe	Salade de tomates	Tomates feta	Tomates feta	Salade de haricots
Tajine d'agneau aux abricots	Barbecue	Côte de porc et légumes	Filet de poisson	Poulet rôti
Semoule bio	Tomates à la Provençale	Boulgour bio	Pâtes bio	Ratatouille
Laitages	Laitages	Laitages	Laitages	Laitages
Tarte au citron	Compote	Tarte tatin	Tarte au citron	Cocktail de fruits
Fruits de saison	Fruits de saison	Fruits de saison	Fruits de saison	
****	****	****	****	****

Bonnes vacances !

1. What options are there for starters on Monday?
2. On which day is *Lemon Pie* a choice for dessert?
3. What are the choices for dessert on Tuesday?
4. What are the choices for the main course on Friday for day students?
5. On which day is fish a choice for the main course?
6. On which day is fruit cocktail a choice for dessert?

Objectifs

● I can read a school canteen menu in French ☐ 😊 😐 ☹

 Research online for Lycée Hoche, a secondary school on the grounds of Versailles Palace. Can you find out about its history? Can you find a school canteen menu?

Mon portfolio 6.1 : Le menu de ma cantine

Faites cet exercice dans votre portfolio. *Do this exercise in your portfolio.*

Au, à la, aux, à l'

In French, when we order foods that include a description of a flavour or topping, we use *à*. However, *à* changes its spelling depending on the gender of the noun that follows and whether it is singular or plural.

- à + le   = **au** (m)   au chocolat
- à + la   = **à la** (f)   à la vanille
- à + l'   = **à l'**   à l'ananas
- à + les = **aux**   aux olives

 Ex. 6.29 La préposition à

Écoutez le CD et complétez les phrases avec la bonne forme de la préposition à. *Listen to the CD and fill in the blanks with the correct form of the preposition à.*

1. Tu bois du café _____ (le lait)?

2. Tu aimes la glace _____ (la vanille)?

3. Vous aimez les crêpes _____ (le chocolat)?

4. Nous mangeons un sandwich _____ (le jambon).

5. J'aime la glace _____ (le Nutella).

6. On aime la glace _____ (la fraise).

7. Vous aimez la pizza _____ (les olives)?

 Ex. 6.30

With your partner, read back over the explanation of the grammar rule behind au, à la, aux *and* à. *Think about the explanation and take turns in explaining it to each other.*

Objectifs

- I understand and can use the prepositions *au, à la, aux* and *à l* _____

Ex. 6.31 Vocabulaire

Écoutez le CD et entrainez-vous à bien prononcer le vocabulaire. Puis, reliez les images avec les bons mots-clés. *Listen to the CD and repeat the vocabulary to improve your pronunciation. Then match each image with a keyword.*

 La glace

- à la vanille
- au chocolat
- au Nutella
- au citron
- à la menthe
- à la pistache
- à la fraise
- à la framboise
- à l'ananas
- au cassis
- au caramel

Le prix

- une boule – 2 euros
- deux boules – 3,50 euros
- trois boules – 5 euros

 Objectifs

- I can read an ice cream parlour menu in French

  Ex. 6.32 Vocabulaire

Écoutez le CD et entrainez-vous à bien prononcer le vocabulaire. *Listen to the CD and repeat the vocabulary to improve your pronunciation.*

Unité 6 : À table

Je voudrais …

- une glace deux boules
- une glace trois boules

- Dans un cornet ou dans un pot ?
- À quel parfum ?
- C'est combien ?

- Ça fait deux euros.
- C'est tout ?
- Oui, c'est tout – merci.

  Ex. 6.33

(a) Écoutez le CD et complétez la conversation avec les mots de l'encadré. *Listen to the CD and fill in the blanks.*

| merci | vanille | au revoir | voilà | chocolat | deux | bonjour |

Vendeuse : _____

Mélodie : Je voudrais une glace _____ boules, s'il vous plait.

Vendeuse : À quel parfum ?

Mélodie : Une boule à la _____ et une boule au

_____, s'il vous plait.

Vendeuse : Dans un cornet ou dans un pot ?

Mélodie : Dans un cornet, s'il vous plait.

Vendeuse : _____, ça fait 3,50 euros, s'il vous plait.

Mélodie : _____, au revoir.

Vendeuse : Je vous en prie. _____.

(b) Vrai ou faux ?

1. Mélodie voudrait trois boules.
2. Elle voudrait une boule au chocolat et une boule à la vanille.
3. Mélodie voudrait un cornet.
4. Ça coûte 3,50 euros.

(c) Reliez les phrases

Une boule à la vanille et	une glace deux boules, s'il vous plait.
Je voudrais	parfum ?
Quel	une boule au chocolat, s'il vous plait.
Dans un cornet	en prie.
Je vous	ou dans un pot ?

Je voudrais *I would like*

Je voudrais is a form of the verb *vouloir*, which means to want. Used as 'Je voudrais', it indicates what you would like or wish for.

It can be followed by a noun or by another verb in the infinitive.

Example:

- Je voudrais *une glace.* (noun)
- Je voudrais *manger* une glace. (verb – infinitive)

 Ex. 6.34

With your partner, think about the infinitive form of verbs. *Can you give two examples of verbs in the infinitive form? What verb form follows verbs such as* je voudrais? *Take turns in explaining and describing this to each other.*

Objectifs

- I understand how *Je voudrais* can be followed by a noun or a verb in the infinitive

  Ex. 6.35 Chez un glacier

Des jeunes vont chez un glacier. *Listen to three young people at an ice cream parlour. Fill in the table.*

	Number of scoops	Flavours	Cone or cup	Price
Julie				
Bertrand				
Jean				

 Ex. 6.36 Jeu de rôle en classe

Carry out a role play with your partner, ordering ice creams *chez le glacier*. Order two ice creams: one with two scoops and one with three scoops. Write out the conversation before you do the role play.

 Ex. 6.37 La lettre d'Aoibhinn

Lisez la lettre d'Aoibhinn, qui est à Collioure chez les Leclerc. Répondez aux questions dans votre cahier. *Read the letter from Aoibhinn, who is staying with the Leclerc family in Collioure. Answer the questions in your copybook.*

Collioure, le 17 juin

Chère Inès,

Un petit coucou du sud de la France ! J'adore la France et je m'amuse bien ici, chez les Leclerc. Ça va, toi ? Tu t'amuses bien pendant les vacances ? Le soleil tape fort ici et il fait très chaud. Collioure est très jolie et le petit port est très mignon. J'adore la cuisine française, et Madame Leclerc est très bonne cuisinière.

Le matin, nous prenons le petit déjeuner ensemble. Normalement, je mange un croissant avec de la confiture et je bois un jus d'orange. Les croissants en France sont super bons ! Il y a aussi des pains au chocolat mais je préfère les croissants.

Le midi, nous déjeunons vers une heure. Comme entrée, en général, il y a de la salade de tomates et comme plat principal, du poisson ou du poulet. Avec le fromage, nous mangeons du pain, de la baguette, hmmm, c'est super bon ! Comme dessert, nous mangeons des fruits. Quelquefois, nous allons au port et nous achetons une glace chez le glacier. C'est incroyable, il y a un tas de parfums !

On a un petit goûter l'après-midi et d'habitude le soir, on dîne vers 7 heures et demie. Toute la famille mange ensemble. Hier soir, en entrée, nous avons mangé de la salade de tomates et de feta. Comme plat principal, nous avons mangé du saumon, après j'ai mangé du camembert et comme dessert, de la mousse au chocolat. Un repas inoubliable ! Je dois dire que j'adore la cuisine française !

Je dois te quitter maintenant. Je vais à la plage cet après-midi. Écris-moi vite ! Je rentre chez moi le 25 juin.

Gros bisous,
Aoibhinn

1. Where in France is Collioure?

2. Name one thing about Collioure that Aoibhinn mentions in her letter.

3. What does Aoibhinn eat for breakfast with the Leclerc family?

4. At what time do they have lunch?

5. What do they usually have for their main course at lunch?

6. What does Aoibhinn buy at the port?

7. Name two things the Leclerc family ate for dinner last night.

8. Where is Aoibhinn going this afternoon?

9. When will she be home?

10. Translate:

cute	
together	
generally	
sometimes	
unbelievable	
lots of	
I must admit	

Objectifs

- I can understand a letter about food culture in France ☐ 😊 😠 😞

Ex. 6.38 Les nombres de 30 à 100

Écoutez le CD et entrainez-vous à bien prononcer le vocabulaire. *Listen to the CD and repeat the vocabulary to improve your pronunciation.*

Les nombres de 30 à 100

30	trente	75	soixante-quinze	88	quatre-vingt-huit
40	quarante	76	soixante-seize	89	quatre-vingt-neuf
41	quarante-et-un	77	soixante-dix-sept	90	quatre-vingt-dix
42	quarante-deux	78	soixante-dix-huit	91	quatre-vingt-onze
50	cinquante	79	soixante-dix-neuf	92	quatre-vingt-douze
51	cinquante-et-un	80	quatre-vingts	93	quatre-vingt-treize
60	soixante	81	quatre-vingt-un	94	quatre-vingt-quatorze
61	soixant-et-un	82	quatre-vingt-deux	95	quatre-vingt-quinze
70	soixante-dix	83	quatre-vingt-trois	96	quatre-vingt-seize
71	soixante-et-onze	84	quatre-vingt-quatre	97	quatre-vingt-dix-sept
72	soixante-douze	85	quatre-vingt-cinq	98	quatre-vingt-dix-huit
73	soixante-treize	86	quatre-vingt-six	99	quatre-vingt-dix-neuf
74	soixante-quatorze	87	quatre-vingt-sept	100	cent

In France, phone numbers are given in pairs, e.g. 01.25.67.34.70

  Ex. 6.39

(a)   **Écoutez le CD et complétez les numéros de téléphone.** *Listen to the CD and fill in the blanks.*

1. 04.☐.55.74.90   **2.** 07.92☐43.20   **3.** 02.52.☐.61.77

(b)   **Écrivez les nombres suivants en lettres.** *Write these numbers in words.*

1. 72 _____ _____
_____ _____

2. 95 _____ _____
_____ _____

3. 83 _____ _____
_____ _____

4. 62 _____ _____
_____ _____

5. 50 _____ _____
_____ _____

6. 45 _____ _____
_____ _____

7. 33 _____ _____
_____ _____

 Visit **www.kahoot.com** to find games to help you practise saying numbers in French.

Objectifs

● I can count from 1 to 100 in French _____ ☐

Ex. 6.40

Lisez la recette et répondez aux questions dans votre cahier. *Read the recipe and answer the questions in your copybook.*

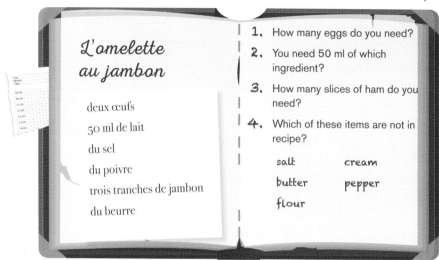

L'omelette au jambon

deux œufs

50 ml de lait

du sel

du poivre

trois tranches de jambon

du beurre

1. How many eggs do you need?
2. You need 50 ml of which ingredient?
3. How many slices of ham do you need?
4. Which of these items are not in recipe?

salt   cream

butter   pepper

flour

Objectifs

- I can read a recipe in French

Ex. 6.41

Reliez les quantités et remplissez les blancs. *Match the ingredients and fill in the blanks.*

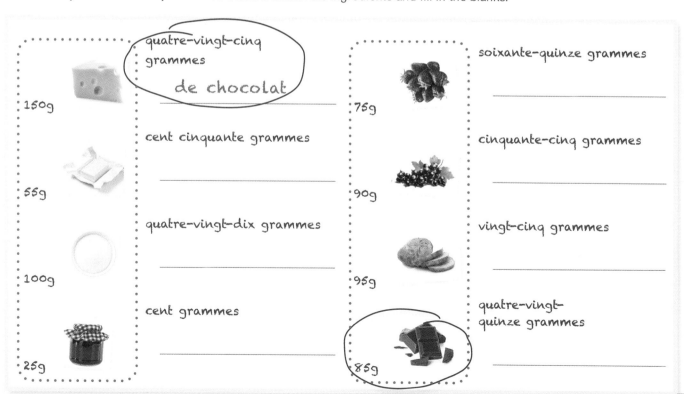

quatre-vingt-cinq grammes
de chocolat

150g

cent cinquante grammes

55g

quatre-vingt-dix grammes

100g

cent grammes

25g

soixante-quinze grammes

75g

cinquante-cinq grammes

90g

vingt-cinq grammes

95g

quatre-vingt-quinze grammes

85g

191

Research Trish Deseine, a food writer from Northern Ireland who is very popular in France and who has had many bestselling books. You could try making one of her recipes, such as French onion soup!

Les verbes en RE   –re verbs

Regular verbs that end in RE are called *re verbs. To use an –re verb in the present tense, you need to do the following:*

1. Knock the –re off the end of the verb: vendre

2. Now you have the stem: vend–

3. Add the correct ending for the subject pronoun, as shown in the table below.

Subject pronouns	Stem	Endings	to sell
Je	vend	s	I sell, I am selling
Tu	vend	s	You sell, You are selling
Il	vend	-	He/it sells, He/it is selling
Elle	vend	-	She/it sells, She/it is selling
On	vend	-	One sells/We sell, One sells/We are selling
Nous	vend	ons	We sell, We are selling
Vous	vend	ez	You sell, You are selling
Ils	vend	ent	They sell, They are selling
Elles	vend	ent	They sell, They are selling

Ex. 6.42 Les verbes en –re

Conjuguez les verbes en –re. Conjugate these –re verbs.

Entendre (to hear)	Attendre (to wait)	Perdre (to lose)
Je		
Tu		
Il/elle		
On		
Nous		
Vous		
Ils/elles		

 Ex. 6.43

Reliez chacun des verbes en –re ci-dessous avec sa traduction en anglais.
Match these –re verbs. Write the verb and its meaning in your copybook.

répondre	to wait
descendre	to lose
tondre	to go down
vendre	to reply
attendre	to sell
entendre	to mow
perdre	to hear

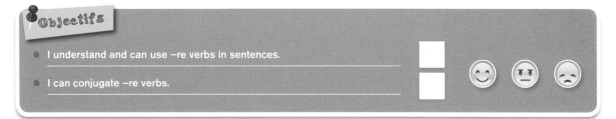

Objectifs

- I understand and can use –re verbs in sentences.
- I can conjugate –re verbs.

Mon portfolio 6.2 : Mon blog sur mes repas

Faites cet exercice dans votre portfolio. *Do this exercise in your portfolio.*

193

Récapitulatif

Mots-clés pour l'Unité 6

Le petit-déjeuner

- le café
- le thé
- le lait
- le jus d'orange
- le sucre

- le chocolat chaud
- un croissant
- le pain grillé
- une tartine
- le pain

- la confiture
- le beurre
- les céréales

Le déjeuner

- une crêpe
- un sandwich
- le jambon
- une salade

- l'huile d'olive
- les œufs
- la soupe
- un croque-monsieur

- un croque-madame
- l'eau

Le diner

- le poulet
- le bœuf
- le poisson

- des légumes
- du riz
- des pâtes

- des frites

Le dessert

- la tarte aux pommes
- le gâteau
- la glace

- une crêpe
- un yaourt
- le fromage

- un fruit

Les quantités

- une tranche de ...
- un morceau de ...

- un litre de ...
- une tasse de ...

- un verre de ...

manger	to eat
Je mange	I eat, I am eating
Tu manges	You eat, You are eating
Il mange	He/it eats, He/it is eating
Elle mange	She/it eats, She/it is eating
On mange	One eats/We eat, One is eating/We are eating
Nous mangeons	We eat, We are eating
Vous mangez	You eat, You are eating
Ils mangent	They eat, They are eating
Elles mangent	They eat, They are eating

boire	to drink
Je bois	I drink, I am drinking
Tu bois	You drink, You are drinking
Il boit	He/it drinks, He/it is drinking
Elle boit	She/it drinks, She/it is drinking
On boit	One drinks/We drink, One is drinking /We are drinking
Nous buvons	We drink, We are drinking
Vous buvez	You drink, You are drinking
Ils boivent	They drink, They are drinking
Elles boivent	They drink, They are drinking

Chez le glacier

- la glace à la vanille
- au chocolat
- au Nutella
- au citron
- à la menthe

- à la pistache
- à la fraise
- à la framboise
- à l'ananas
- au cassis

- au caramel
- le prix
- une boule – 2 euros
- deux boules – 3,50 euros
- trois boules – 5 euros

Je voudrais

- une glace deux boules
- une glace trois boules
- Dans un cornet ou dans un pot ?

- À quel parfum ?
- C'est combien ?
- Ça fait deux euros.

- C'est tout ?
- Oui, c'est tout – merci.

Les nombres de 30 à 100

30	trente		82	quatre-vingt-deux
40	quarante		83	quatre-vingt-trois
41	quarante-et-un		84	quatre-vingt-quatre
42	quarante-deux		85	quatre-vingt-cinq
50	cinquante		86	quatre-vingt-six
51	cinquante-et-un		87	quatre-vingt-sept
60	soixante		88	quatre-vingt-huit
61	soixant-et-un		89	quatre-vingt-neuf
70	soixante-dix		90	quatre-vingt-dix
71	soixante-et-onze		91	quatre-vingt-onze
72	soixante-douze		92	quatre-vingt-douze
73	soixante-treize		93	quatre-vingt-treize
74	soixante-quatorze		94	quatre-vingt-quatorze
75	soixante-quinze		95	quatre-vingt-quinze
76	soixante-seize		96	quatre-vingt-seize
77	soixante-dix-sept		97	quatre-vingt-dix-sept
78	soixante-dix-huit		98	quatre-vingt-dix-huit
79	soixante-dix-neuf		99	quatre-vingt-dix-neuf
80	quatre-vingts		100	cent
81	quatre-vingt-un			

Bilan de l'Unité 6. *Checklist for Unit 6.*

Pour chaque objectif, choisissez votre émoticône.	😊	😐	😞
Listening			
I can understand when people list what they eat at mealtimes			
I can understand a simple shopping list			
I can understand when people give their opinions on food and meals in a small group			
I can understand the flavours of ice creams			
I can understand quantities in numbers			
I can understand descriptions of quantities such as a slice or a piece			
I can understand prices of items			
I can understand a phone number in French			
Reading			
I can read a short blog about people's mealtimes			
I can read a short letter about meals and food culture in France			
I can read a weekly lunch menu for a school			
I can read a menu from an ice cream parlour			
I can read a short role play, ordering an ice cream			
I can read the numbers 1 to 100 and recognise them when they are used in a list of ingredients			
I can read the ingredients of a simple dish			
Spoken production			
I can say what I have for breakfast, lunch, dinner and dessert			
I can say what foods I like			
I can say what ice cream flavours I like			
I can count from 1 to 100			

Unité 6 : À table

I can say a phone number in French			
I can ask for a slice, piece or simple quantity of a food			
Spoken interaction			
I can ask someone what they eat for each meal			
I can ask for an ice cream, including the flavour and number of scoops			
I can carry out a short role play at the ice cream parlour			
I can respond to someone's opinion about the foods they like or dislike			
Writing			
I can write short answers to questions about meals and foods			
I can write a short blog about my meals and food choices			
I can write a letter to my pen pal about mealtimes in Ireland			
I can write a weekly lunch menu for my school canteen			
I can write a role play at an ice cream parlour			

Discutez en classe. *Have a class discussion.*

- Look back over your Portfolio exercises. In which areas did you give yourself stars?
- Look at your wishes. Have any of these improved?
- What was your favourite part of Unité 6? Why?
- What did you least enjoy in Unité 6? Why?
- Think about the next unit you will work on. What are you looking forward to learning more about? Why?

1. **Lisez le passage et répondez aux questions dans votre cahier.** *Read the extract and answer the questions in your copybook.*

> Salut, je m'appelle Benjamin et je suis français. Ma mère s'appelle Chris et elle est suédoise, mon pere s'appelle Jérôme et il est français. Je n'ai ni frères ni sœurs mais j'ai beaucoup de cousins ici en France et aussi en Suède. Cet été était inoubliable avec l'Euro 2016. Moi et mes cousins sommes allés voir le match de la Suède contre l'Irlande. Le Stade de France est magnifique. La Suède a bien joué, surtout mon joueur préféré Zlatan. Je suis fan de foot ! Je joue avec mon équipe locale sur le terrain de foot près de chez moi. Nous nous entrainons deux fois par semaine. Je joue au foot depuis 8 ans.

1. Where is Benjamin from?
2. What nationality is his mum?
3. Why was last summer unforgettable?
4. Which match did Benjamin go to?
5. Who went with him?
6. Where was it?
7. Who is Zlatan?
8. Where does Benjamin train?
9. How often does he train?
10. How long has he been playing football?

 2. **Faites des recherches sur Internet puis répondez aux questions dans votre cahier.** *Research online, then answer the questions in your copybook.*

1. Name three sports that are popular in France.
2. Find out where in France each sport is played or takes place.
3. Name one famous athlete associated with each sport.
4. Find three interesting facts about each of the sports.
5. Prepare a 'culture presentation' for your class, using the information you gathered during your research. Your final presentation can be a poster or a PowerPoint slideshow. Include ten keywords in French.

 3. **Complétez les phrases avec la bonne forme de l'article partitif.** *Fill in the blanks with the correct form of* l'article partitif.

1. Je bois _____ (de la/du) café au lait.
2. Il boit _____ (du/de l') jus d'orange.
3. Il mange _____ (du/des) bœuf.
4. Nous mangeons _____ (du/de la) pain grillé avec _____ (des/du) beurre.
5. Tu manges _____ (des/du) croissants.

 4. **(A)** **Écrivez un menu pour l'anniversaire de votre ami(e) (entrée, plat principal, dessert, boissons).** *Write a menu for your friend's birthday (starter, main course, dessert, drinks). You can draw your menu as a poster or use your computer to design it. Give the menu a birthday theme.*

(B) **Écrivez une lettre à votre ami(e).** *Write a letter to your friend.*
- Tell them what sports you play.
- Tell them when and where you play sports.
- Ask them what sports they like to play.

5. Jeu de plateau. *Board game.*

You will need:

- A different coloured counter for each player
- A dice

Rules

- 2–5 players
- The youngest player rolls first, the second-youngest rolls second, etc.
- Roll the dice and move on that number of squares.
- Take the challenge on your square.
- If you give an incorrect answer, you miss a turn.
- The first player to reach 'Vous avez gagné' wins the game!

Astuces

Try to use as much French as possible during the game. Here are some useful phrases.

Commençons !	Let's begin!
À moi !	My turn!
À toi !	Your turn!
Lance le dé !	Throw the dice!
Avance d'une case !	Move forward one square!
Recule d'une case !	Go back one square!

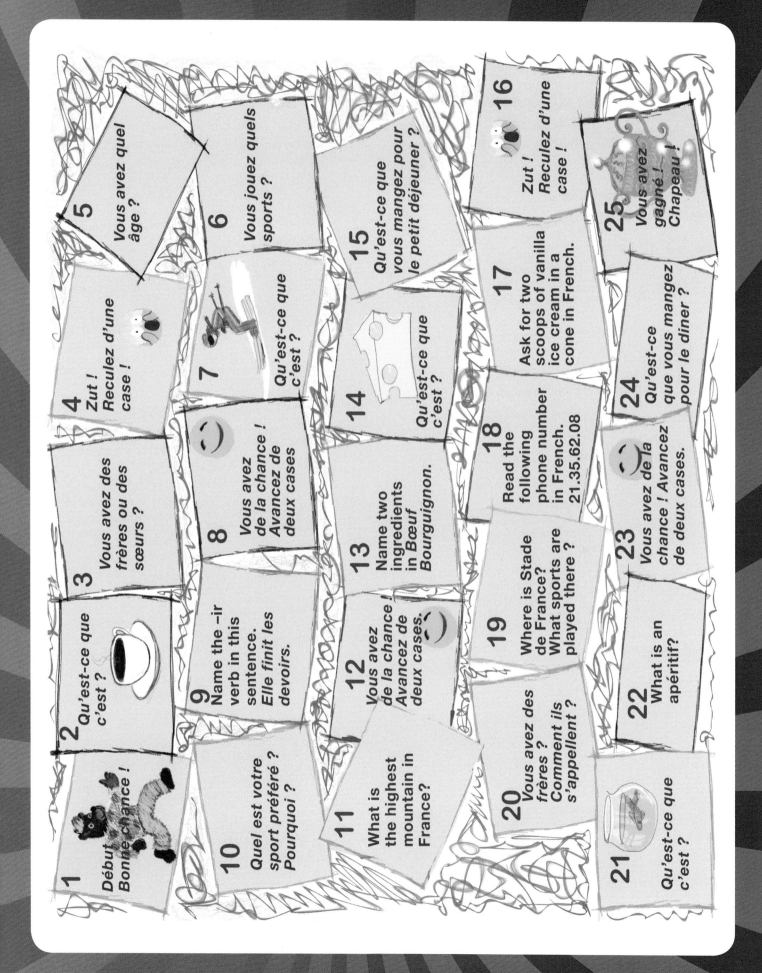

1 Début Bonne chance !

2 Qu'est-ce que c'est ?

3 Vous avez des frères ou des sœurs ?

4 Zut ! Reculez d'une case !

5 Vous avez quel âge ?

6 Vous jouez quels sports ?

7 Qu'est-ce que c'est ?

8 Vous avez de la chance ! Avancez de deux cases

9 Name the -ir verb in this sentence. Elle finit les devoirs.

10 Quel est votre sport préféré ? Pourquoi ?

11 What is the highest mountain in France?

12 Vous avez de la chance ! Avancez de deux cases.

13 Name two ingredients in Bœuf Bourguignon.

14 Qu'est-ce que c'est ?

15 Qu'est-ce que vous mangez pour le petit déjeuner ?

16 Zut ! Reculez d'une case !

17 Ask for two scoops of vanilla ice cream in a cone in French.

18 Read the following phone number in French. 21.35.62.08

19 Where is Stade de France? What sports are played there ?

20 Vous avez des frères ? Comment ils s'appellent ?

21 Qu'est-ce que c'est ?

22 What is an apéritif?

23 Vous avez de la chance ! Avancez de deux cases.

24 Qu'est-ce que vous mangez pour le dîner ?

25 Vous avez gagné ! Chapeau !

201

6. **Une petite pièce de théâtre !** *A little piece of theatre play!*

Below is the script for a short play. Act it out in small groups. It's a great way to practise your new vocabulary. Audience members can take notes to help the actors improve on their pronunciation!

Présentation

Les jeunes vont au terrain de foot. Ils ont un ballon.

Liste des des personnages

- Claire
- Emma

- Benjamin
- David

Emma, Benjamin, David :
　Salut, Claire. Ça va ?

Claire : Oui, ça va. Et vous ?

Benjamin : Ça va bien.

Emma et David :
　Oui, ça va.

Claire : On va au terrain de foot ?

Emma : Oui, j'ai apporté mon ballon.

David et Benjamin :
　Bonne idée, Claire.

David : Merci, Emma !

Emma : Nous avons un match de foot samedi prochain contre le lycée Valentin.

Claire : Emma a marqué un beau but pendant le dernier match contre le lycée Valentin, mais on a quand même perdu.

Emma : Oui, mais samedi prochain, on va gagner !

David : Oui, tu joues bien au foot, Emma, et toi aussi Claire. Allez, on y va ? Passe-moi le ballon, Emma !

Benjamin : Oui, je suis d'accord, vous jouez super bien toutes les deux. On y va !

UNITÉ 7

Une journée au collège

ÉCOLE

peach
pêche

lemon
citron

apple
pomme

Parlez-vous Français?

By the end of this unit you will

- Name the different facilities in your school
- Draw a map of your school and label the different facilities and offices on it
- Give a tour of your school and give your opinion of the school
- Name your school subjects and give your opinion on them
- Understand a school timetable
- Ask and tell the time in French
- Understand and use the 24-hour clock in French
- Talk about a typical day and your routine for going to school

Ex. 7.1 La Vie en France

Regardez la vidéo et répondez aux questions. *Watch the video and answer the questions.*

1. What is *la Toussaint*?
2. How many school zones are there in France?
3. How do the different zones affect school holidays?
4. Is the school day longer in Ireland or in France?
5. Name three subjects that French students learn.

 Objectifs

• I can explain some differences and similarities between school in France and school in Ireland ☺ 😐 ☹

Ex. 7.2 Vocabulaire

Écoutez le CD et entraînez-vous à bien prononcer le vocabulaire. Puis, reliez les images avec les bons mots-clés. *Listen to the CD and repeat the vocabulary to improve your pronunciation. Then match each image with a keyword.*

Mon collège et ses équipements

- la salle de classe
- la cantine
- le bureau du principal
- le bureau du principal-adjoint
- le laboratoire
- le gymnase
- la cour de récréation
- la réception
- la bibliothèque
- la salle de cuisine
- le couloir
- la salle d'informatique
- le terrain de foot

 Objectifs

• I can name school facilities in French ☺ 😐 ☹

 **Ex. 7.3**

Traduisez les mots et cherchez-les dans les mots cachés. *Translate the words and find them in the word search.*

Anglais	Français
classroom	
laboratory	
gymnasium	
principal's office	

Anglais	Français
canteen	
computer room	
library	
school yard	

O	H	W	O	L	L	J	L	P	F	Q	C	M	E	E	L	F	X	A	Z
I	E	Q	C	J	E	V	M	M	S	S	N	P	U	U	A	Y	S	N	K
B	R	U	K	W	E	G	C	P	I	W	W	Y	Q	Q	C	Q	D	R	A
E	Q	Z	V	V	O	Y	Y	C	P	V	O	E	I	O	L	V	F	N
I	C	Y	Y	O	I	X	K	M	I	P	H	Q	H	T	U	R	V	C	A
K	J	T	P	L	D	B	E	N	N	V	M	Q	T	A	R	X	L	P	T
M	B	R	X	F	W	T	H	K	K	A	V	I	O	M	D	Y	C	E	H
B	Y	H	E	U	Q	R	X	O	W	Y	S	P	I	R	E	X	P	P	J
L	E	L	A	B	O	R	A	T	O	I	R	E	L	O	R	S	C	L	B
L	W	P	M	S	U	V	U	C	X	V	C	J	B	F	E	V	C	J	P
C	L	E	B	U	R	E	A	U	D	U	P	R	I	N	C	I	P	A	L
R	Q	X	G	P	G	D	H	D	R	E	T	P	B	I	R	L	F	Z	H
H	H	J	I	S	V	V	H	Z	S	M	P	M	A	D	E	A	Y	N	N
B	Q	R	M	W	J	G	Q	C	Y	Z	N	P	L	E	A	C	E	K	F
E	S	S	A	L	C	E	D	E	L	L	A	S	A	L	T	A	U	A	P
M	X	E	T	I	M	L	N	U	Y	R	D	Z	Q	L	I	N	E	C	E
C	S	X	P	J	L	H	Z	V	Q	L	R	Y	Y	A	O	T	M	V	V
S	O	Z	H	N	R	X	U	J	F	L	J	O	G	S	N	I	V	T	C
T	G	X	M	I	R	R	M	R	R	S	J	F	W	A	V	N	C	W	J
H	H	C	N	M	U	H	Z	D	A	J	X	G	G	L	L	E	P	P	H

Chloé et Jean parlent de leur collège et disent s'il est bien équipé. *Chloé and Jean talk about their schools and their facilities.*

(a) Écoutez le CD et complétez les deux textes. Listen to the CD and fill in the blanks.

Chloé Salut, je m'appelle Chloé et j'ai 13 _____. Je vais

_____ Collège Jules Vernes, qui se trouve à Nice. Mon collège

est très _____, il y a environ deux milles élèves, et c'est

_____. Mon collège est _____

équipé, par exemple, il y a _____, une cantine, des laboratoires, une belle

_____, un gymnase et _____. Tout est très

_____. J'aime bien mon collège.

Jean Salut, je m'appelle Jean et je _____ au Collège Claude Monet,

_____ Normandie. La Normandie se trouve dans le nord-ouest

de la France. C'est un collège mixte et il y a _____ d'élèves.

Ce n'est _____ un collège très moderne, en fait il est assez

_____. Mais les _____ sont assez

bien, surtout la _____. Les menus sont en ligne et en général, c'est

très bon. Nous avons aussi une grande bibliothèque, une cour de récréation assez sympa, un gymnase et

_____.

(b) True or false?

Chloé

1. Her school is small.

2. It is a mixed school.

3. Chloé doesn't like her school.

4. There is no library in her school.

Jean

1. His school is in Paris.

2. His school is very modern.

3. His school is mixed.

4. His school has a library and laboratories.

(c) Translate:

I like my school.		canteen	
a mixed school		laboratory	
good facilities		gym	
library		yard	

Objectifs

- I can read and understand a short description about a school _____

Mon portfolio 7. 1 : Ma matière préférée

Faites cet exercice dans votre portfolio. *Do this exercise in your portfolio.*

 Ex. 7.5 Mon collège

Complétez les phrases suivantes pour parler de votre collège. *Fill in the blanks with information about your school.*

1. Mon collège s'appelle _____.

2. Mon collège se trouve à _____.

3. C'est une _____ (école mixte/école de filles/école de garçons).

4. Mon collège est _____ (moderne/vieux/assez moderne/assez vieux).

5. Mon collège est bien équipé; par exemple, il y a _____.

   _____, _____.

6. Il n'y a pas de _____.

Objectifs

- I can write a short description of my own school in French _____

Ex. 7.6 Vocabulaire

(a) **Écoutez le CD et entrainez-vous à bien prononcer le vocabulaire. Puis, reliez les images avec les bons mot-clés.** *Listen to the CD and repeat the vocabulary to improve your pronunciation. Then match each image with a keyword.*

Les matières

- l'anglais
- le français
- le gaélique
- l'allemand
- l'espagnol
- l'italien

- les maths
- la géographie
- l'histoire
- l'économie
- les sciences (de la Vie et de la Terre)

- la musique
- l'éducation physique
- l'éducation civique
- l'informatique
- l'art

- la technologie
- l'éducation religieuse

 (b) **Des jeunes décrivent leurs matières préférées. Complétez le tableau suivant.** *The teenagers describe their favourite subjects. Write the information into the correct column.*

	Subjects studied	Favourite subjects
Jake		
Emma		
Ava		

 Objectifs

- I can recognise my school subjects in French when I hear them
- I can name my school subjects in French

 Ex. 7.7 À deux

À deux : posez les questions à votre camarade et répondez à ses questions. Complétez la grille. *Talk with your classmate. Ask them questions and reply to theirs. Fill in the grid with your answers and theirs.*

Questions	Mes réponses	Les réponses de ma/mon camarade
Tu étudies quelles matières ?	J'étudie …	
C'est quoi ta matière préférée ?	Ma matière préférée, c'est …	
Qu'est-ce que tu manges au gouter ?		
Qu'est-ce que tu manges le soir, au diner ?		

Objectifs

- I can ask someone which subjects they study _____
- I can answer a question about the subjects I study

Ex. 7.8 Interévaluation

First, fill in the grid below for yourself, then work with a partner to provide each other with feedback on your performances in Ex. 7.7.

Words I knew really well	
Words I didn't know	
Words I need to pronounce better	
Words I pronounced really well	
My intonation	

Ex. 7.9 Vocabulaire

Écoutez le CD et entrainez-vous à bien prononcer le vocabulaire. *Listen to the CD and repeat the vocabulary to improve your pronunciation.*

 Mes opinions

- J'aime bien
- Je n'aime pas
- C'est nul.
- C'est cool.

- C'est intéressant.
- C'est ennuyeux.
- C'est difficile.
- C'est facile.

- C'est ma matière préférée.
- C'est créatif et amusant.

  # Ex. 7.10

Martha et Benoît parlent de leurs matières préférées. *Martha and Benoit talk about their favourite subjects.*

(a) Écoutez le CD et complétez les textes. *Listen to the CD and fill in the blanks.*

Martha

J'étudie _____, l'anglais, _____,

les sciences, _____ et la technologie. Ma matière préférée, c'est

_____ parce que c'est _____ et utile.

Je n'aime pas _____ parce que c'est nul et ennuyeux. Le français est moins intéressant que l'anglais. L'anglais est plus utile que le français.

Benoît

Je fais _____, informatique, _____,

SVT (Sciences de la Vie et de la Terre), _____, géographie et

_____. Mon emploi du _____ est très

chargé. J'aime bien _____ et _____.

Ma matière préférée, c'est _____ parce que c'est intéressant et

_____. Je n'aime pas _____ parce que c'est

_____ et on a trop de devoirs ! L'anglais est moins facile que les maths. Les maths sont plus utiles que l'anglais.

(b)

1. What is Martha's favourite subject? Why?

2. What subject does Martha not like? Why?

3. What is Benoît's favourite subject? Why?

4. What subject does Benoît not like? Why?

(c) **Translate:**

I study	
My favourite subject is	
It is interesting	
My timetable is very busy.	
We have too much homework.	
because	
interesting	
and	

(d) Find one example of each of the following:

A masculine definite article _____

A feminine possessive adjective _____

A masculine adjective _____

A regular verb _____

An irregular verb _____

 Objectifs

● I can read a short description from a student about their school subjects _____

 Plus … que *or* **Moins … que**

We use *plus* (more) and *moins* (less) when we compare things.

- Le français est plus intéressant que l'anglais.
- La géo est plus difficile que l'histoire.
- L'EPS, c'est plus amusant que la technologie.
- La technologie est plus utile que les sciences.

- Le français est moins utile que la technologie.
- La géo, c'est moins intéressant que l'histoire.

Ex. 7.11

With your partner, think about the grammar rule behind *plus … que* and *moins … que*. *Take turns in explaining and describing this to each other.*

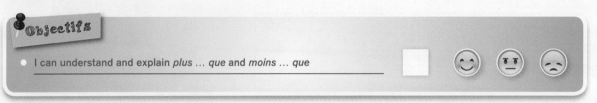

Objectifs

● I can understand and explain *plus … que* and *moins … que* _____

Ex. 7.12

Écrivez votre opinion sur les matières suivantes dans votre cahier. *Write your opinion on the following subjects in your copybook.*

- ● l'anglais
- ● le gaélique
- ● le français

- ● l'histoire
- ● la géographie

Objectifs

● I can give my opinion of school subjects in French _____

Astuces

Extend your answers by using words and phrases such as *parce que* (because), *et* (and) and *mais* (but).

For example: someone asks *C'est quoi ta matière préférée ?*

You could say *J'aime bien l'anglais*. This is a clear answer but it doesn't give much information. You could say instead:

- ● *J'aime bien l'anglais parce que c'est intéressant.*
- ● *J'aime bien l'anglais parce que c'est intéressant et utile.*
- ● *J'aime bien l'anglais parce que c'est intéressant et utile, mais ce n'est pas très facile.*

Ex. 7.13 À deux

À deux: posez la question à votre camarade et répondez à sa question 'C'est quoi ta matière préférée ?' Utilisez *parce que*, *et*, *mais* pour donner votre opinion. *Talk with your classmate. Ask them this question and reply to theirs: What is your favourite subject? Use* parce que, et *and* mais *to give your opinion on the subjects in Ex. 7.12.*

Objectifs

- I can use *parce que*, *et* and *mais* to extend my sentences and give more information

Mon portfolio 7. 2 : Mon emploi du temps

Faites cet exercice dans votre portfolio. *Do this exercise in your portfolio.*

Ex. 7.14 Vocabulaire

Écoutez le CD et entrainez-vous à bien prononcer le vocabulaire. *Listen to the CD and repeat the vocabulary to improve your pronunciation.*

Il est quelle heure?			...	et quart	10:15
Il est dix heures	10:00		...	vingt	10:20
Il est dix heures cinq	10:05		...	vingt-cinq	10:25
Il est dix heures dix	10:10		...	trente/et demie	10:30

Objectifs

- I can understand the time for the first half of the clock when I hear it in French
- I can tell the time in French for the first half of the clock

 **Ex. 7.15**

Reliez les phrases avec les images qui correspondent. *Match each phrase with the correct image.*

1. Il est trois heures.

 a.

2. Il est une heure et quart.

 b.

3. Il est cinq heures vingt.

 c.

4. Il est huit heures cinq.

 d.

5. Il est dix heures dix.

 e.

  Ex. 7.16

Écoutez le CD et écrivez l'heure indiquée. *Listen to the CD and write the correct time.*

1. _____   4. _____

2. _____   5. _____

3. _____   6. _____

Ex. 7.17 Vocabulaire

Écoutez le CD et entrainez-vous à bien prononcer le vocabulaire. *Listen to the CD and repeat the vocabulary to improve your pronunciation.*

• Il est onze heures	11:00	• ... moins le quart	10:45
• ... moins vingt-cinq	10:35	• ... moins dix.	10:50
• ... moins vingt	10:40	• ... moins cinq	10:55

 Ex. 7.18

Reliez les phrases avec les images qui correspondent. *Match each phrase with the correct image.*

1. Il est neuf heures moins le quart.

2. Il est huit heures et demie.

3. Il est sept heures moins le quart.

4. Il est dix heures moins vingt.

5. Il est sept heures moins cinq.

6. Il est trois heures vingt.

7. Il est quatre heures dix.

8. Il est une heure vingt-cinq.

9. Il est six heures moins cinq.

10. Il est neuf heures vingt.

a.

b.

c.

d.

e.

f.

g.

h.

i.

j.

Objectifs

- I can tell the time in French
- I can ask what time it is in French

Astuces

The **24-hour clock** is used frequently in France.

- The **a.m. hours** are 1:00, 2:00, 3:00, 4:00, 5:00, 6:00, 7:00, 8:00, 9:00, 10:00, 11:00
- **Noon** is 12:00
- The **p.m. hours** are:
  13:00 (1 p.m.)
  14:00 (2 p.m.)
  15:00 (3 p.m.)
  16:00 (4 p.m.)

17:00 (5 p.m.)
18:00 (6 p.m.)
19:00 (7 p.m.)
20:00 (8 p.m.)
21:00 (9 p.m.)
22:00 (10 p.m.)
23:00 (11 p.m.)

- **Midnight** is 00:00

Objectifs

- I can understand the 24-hour clock

Ex. 7.19 L'emploi du temps de Stéphanie

Regardez l'emploi du temps de Stéphanie et répondez aux questions. *Look at Stéphanie's timetable and answer the questions.*

	LUNDI	MARDI	MERCREDI	JEUDI	VENDREDI
8h30	français	géo	histoire	EPS	SVT
9h30	français	maths	anglais	SVT	maths
10h20 récréation					
10h30	maths	géo	maths	SVT	français
11h30	SVT	français	technologie	maths	technologie
12h30 déjeuner					
14h10	musique	musique		géo	SVT
15h10	technologie	SVT		français	géo
16h 10	géo	anglais		musique	EPS
17h10 fin des cours					

(a) **Trouvez les paires.** *Find the pairs.*

Le lundi à neuf heures et demie,	j'ai SVT.
Le lundi à seize heures dix,	j'ai français.
Le mardi à onze heures trente,	j'ai français.
Le mardi à quinze heures dix,	j'ai maths.
Le jeudi à huit heures et demie,	j'ai histoire.
Le jeudi à seize heures dix,	j'ai géo.
Le vendredi à quinze heures dix,	j'ai EPS.
Le vendredi à seize heures dix,	j'ai géo.
Le mercredi à huit heures et demie,	j'ai EPS.
Le mercredi à dix heures et demie,	j'ai musique

(b)

1. At what time is French on a Monday?
2. What time is Maths on a Thursday?
3. What days is PE?
4. How many English classes has Stéphanie each week?
5. What time does school start?
6. What time is morning break?
7. What time is lunch?
8. How long does the lunch break last?
9. What time does school finish?
10. How many classes does Stéphanie have each day?
11. What time is school over on a Wednesday?
12. How many classes does Stéphanie have on a Wednesday?

 Objectifs

- I can read a school timetable in French

 **Ex. 7.20 À deux**

À deux : posez les questions à votre camarade et répondez à ses questions. **Complétez la grille.** *Talk with your classmate. Ask them questions and reply to theirs. Fill in the grid with your answers and theirs.*

Questions	Mes réponses	Les réponses de ma/ mon camarade
Que fait Stéphanie le lundi à neuf heures trente ?		
Que fait Stéphanie le mardi à neuf heures trente ?		
Que fait Stéphanie le jeudi à quatre heures dix ?		
Que fait Stéphanie le vendredi à 14h10 ?		

Objectifs

• I can read and talk about a school timetable in French _____

Ex. 7.21 Interévaluation

First, fill in the grid below for yourself, then work with a partner to provide each other with feedback on your performances in Ex. 7.20.

Words I knew really well	
Words I didn't know	
Words I need to pronounce better	
Words I pronounced really well	
My intonation	

Mon portfolio 7.3 : Mon blog sur une journée typique

Faites cet exercice dans votre portfolio. *Do this exercise in your portfolio.*

  Ex. 7.22

Écoutez le CD et entrainez-vous à bien prononcer le vocabulaire. Puis, reliez les images avec les bons mots-clés.
Listen to the CD and repeat the vocabulary to improve your pronunciation. Then match each image with the correct keyword.

 Une journée typique

1. Je me lève
2. Je me lave
3. Je m'habille
4. Je prends mon petit déjeuner
5. Je quitte la maison
6. J'arrive
7. Les cours commencent
8. Je déjeune
9. Les cours finissent
10. Je rentre

a.

b.

c.

d.

e.

f.

g.

h.

i.

j.

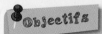

- I can read and understand the keywords for a typical day

Les verbes pronominaux *Reflexive verbs*

Did you notice that the verbs we learned for a typical day look a little different from the verbs we've met before? For example: in *Je me lève* you can see that there are two parts to the verb. This is because it is a **reflexive verb**.

We use reflexive verbs when the person doing the action is doing it to themselves. Reflexive verbs use an extra pronoun (called a *reflexive pronoun*). In *Je **me** lève*, the reflexive pronoun is *me*.

Reflexive verbs don't work in quite the same way in English as they do in French. The closest English-language equivalent is when we use the word *myself* with a verb.

- I wash (myself)   *Je me lave*
- I dress (myself)   *Je m'habille*

In English, we don't need to use *myself* for these sentences to make sense. In French, we need to use *me* (the reflexive pronoun).

These are the reflexive pronouns in French.

Je	me	myself
Tu	te	yourself
Il	se	himself
Ell	se	herself
On	se	oneself/ourselves

Nous nous	ourselves
Vous vous	yourself/ yourselves
Ils se	themselves
Elles se	themselves

Let's look at some reflexive verbs in action!

I get up in French is   *Je me lève*.

The verb is *lever* and it is an –*er* verb, so it takes the normal –*er* verb endings. We just need to remember to use the reflexive pronoun with it.

Remember the –*er* verb endings:

Je	e
Tu	es
Il/elle/on	e

Nous	ons
Vous	ez
Ils/elles	ent

When we want to use a reflexive verb, we need to remember three parts.

Écoutez le CD et entrainez-vous à bien prononcer le vocabulaire. *Listen to the CD and repeat the vocabulary to improve your pronunciation.*

1. Subject pronoun	2. Reflexive pronoun	3. Verb
Je	me	lève
Tu	te	lèves
Il/elle/on	se	lève
Nous	nous	levons
Vous	vous	levez
Ils/elles	se	lèvent

 Ex. 7.23

Complétez la grille pour le verbe *se laver*. *Fill in the verb* se laver.

1. Subject pronoun	2. Reflexive pronoun	3. Verb
Je	me	
	te	laves
Il/elle/on		
	nous	lavons
Vous		
Ils/elles		lavent

 Ex. 7.24

With your partner, think about reflexive verbs. *Take turns in answering and explaining these questions:*

1. What is a reflexive verb?

2. How do you form a reflexive verb?

3. How many words are used when we use a reflexive verb in French?

4. What endings do reflexive verbs take?

 Objectifs

- I understand and can explain reflexive verbs in French _____

Ex. 7.25 Ma journée typique

Écoutez le CD et reliez les phrases avec les images qui correspondent. *Listen to the CD and match each phrase with the correct image.*

1. Je me lève à sept heures.

2. Je me lave à sept heures dix.

3. Je m'habille à sept heures vingt.

4. Je prends le petit déjeuner à sept heures et demie.

5. Je quitte la maison à huit heures.

7. Les cours commencent à neuf heures.

8. J'ai une récré à onze heures.

10. Les cours finissent à trois heures et demie.

11. Je rentre chez moi à

a.

b.

c.

d.

e.

f.

g.

h.

i.

j.

k.

Ex. 7.26

Décrivez votre journée typique. Écrivez une phrase pour chaque image. Utilisez les verbes et écrivez l'heure.
Describe a typical day for you. Write one phrase for each image below. Use the verbs and write the time.

1. s'habiller
2. quitter
3. se laver
4. finir
5. déjeuner
   manger/
   prendre
6. rentrer
7. arriver
8. se lever

 a.

 e.

 b.

 f.

 c.

g.

 d.

 h.

Unité 7 : Une journée au collège

Ex. 7.27 La journée typique d'Élodie

Écoutez et lisez : Élodie raconte sa journée typique. *Listen to and read what Élodie says about her typical day.*

(a) **Écoutez le CD et complétez le texte.** *Listen to the CD and fill in the blanks.*

Salut, je _____. Élodie, j'ai _____ ans

et j'habite à Montréal, au _____. Je parle anglais et français. Je vais au

_____ St Germain, à Montréal. _____ bien

mon collège. Il est _____, il y a beaucoup d'élèves et il est super bien équipé :

il y a un grand _____, des _____ de sports,

une piscine, des laboratoires modernes _____.

Je _____ à six heures et demie. Je _____

immédiatement. D'abord, je _____ et puis je m'habille. À

_____, je prends le petit déjeuner, c'est-à-dire du pain grillé et du jus

d'orange. Je quitte la maison à _____et je vais au collège. Les cours

commencent à _____. Nous avons une petite récré à onze heures et le

déjeuner est à une heure. Les cours finissent à trois heures et demie. Je rentre chez moi à quatre heures. À la

maison, je fais d'abord _____ puis après ça, j'aime bien aller jouer au basket

_____ mes amis.

(b) **Trouvez les paires.** *Find the pairs.*

Je parle	c'est-à-dire du pain grillé et du jus d'orange.
Je vais	mes devoirs.
Le collège /cégep est	à huit heures.
Je me réveille	à cinq heures et demie.
Les cours commencent	anglais et français.
Je prends le petit déjeuner	à six heures et demie.
Je rentre chez moi	super bien équipé.
À la maison, je fais	au collège St Germain

224

(c)

1. How old is Élodie?
2. Where does she live?
3. Name three facilities at her school.
4. At what time does she get up?
5. At what time does she have breakfast?
6. What does she have for breakfast?
7. At what time do classes start?
8. When does she have her morning break?
9. At what time does she get home from school?
10. What does she do after her homework?

(d) Translate:

I like my school	
with	
lots of students	
facilities	

immediately	
firstly	
after that	
then	

(e) Find one example of each of the following:

Avoir _____

Être _____

Feminine adjective _____

Objectifs

- I can read and understand a detailed description of a student's typical day at school _____ ☐

Mon portfolio 7.4 : Le tour guidé de mon collège

Faites cet exercice dans votre portfolio. *Do this exercise in your portfolio.*

Mots-clés pour l'Unité 7

Mon collège et ses équipements

- la salle de classe
- la cantine
- le bureau du principal
- le bureau du principal-adjoint
- le laboratoire

- le gymnase
- la cour de récréation
- la réception
- la bibliothèque
- la salle de cuisine

- le couloir
- la salle d'informatique
- le terrain de foot

Les matières

- l'anglais
- le français
- le gaélique
- l'allemand
- l'espagnol
- l'italien
- les maths

- la géographie
- l'histoire
- l'économie
- les sciences (de la Vie et de la Terre)
- la musique
- l'éducation physique

- l'éducation civique
- l'informatique
- l'art
- la technologie
- l'éducation religieuse

Mes opinions

- J'aime bien
- Je n'aime pas
- C'est nul.
- C'est cool.

- C'est intéressant.
- C'est ennuyeux.
- C'est difficile.
- C'est facile.

- C'est ma matière préférée.
- C'est créatif et amusant.

Il est quelle heure ?

			...	et quart	10:15
Il est dix heures.	10:00		...	vingt	10:20
Il est dix heures cinq.	10:05		...	vingt-cinq	10:25
Il est dix heures dix.	10:10		...	trente/et demie	10:30
Il est onze heures	11:00		...	moins le quart	10:45
... moins vingt-cinq	10:35		...	moins dix	10:50
... moins vingt	10:40		...	moins cinq	10:55

Une journée typique

- Je me lève
- Je me lave
- Je m'habille
- Je prends mon petit déjeuner

- Je quitte la maison
- J'arrive
- Les cours commencent
- Je déjeune

- Les cours finissent
- Je rentre

Bilan de l'Unité 7. *Checklist for Unit 7.*

Pour chaque objectif, choisissez votre émoticône.	😊	😐	😞
Listening			
I can understand someone naming the facilities in their school			
I can understand someone giving a tour of their school building, when they speak slowly			
I can understand someone naming their school subjects			
I can understand someone giving a brief opinion on school subjects			
I can understand someone telling me their favourite school subject, and why they like it			
I can understand someone telling the time			
I can understand someone telling the time using the 24-hour clock			
I can understand someone giving a brief description of their typical day			
Reading			
I can read signs for different locations in my school building			
I can read a short description of a school and its facilities			
I can read the names of school subjects on books			
I can read a school timetable in French			
I can read a blog about school in France			
I can read a short paragraph about a person's typical day			
Spoken production			
I can name the facilities in my school			
I can give a short tour of my school building			
I can name my school subjects			
I can say which is my favourite subject and why			
I can describe my typical day in a few sentences			

Unité 7 : Une journée au collège

Spoken interaction			
I can ask someone what their school is like			
I can ask someone what subjects they study, which is their favourite, and why			
I can ask the time in French			
I can tell the time in French			
I can ask someone about their daily routine			
I can answer questions about my daily routine			
Writing			
I can write signs to name the facilities in my school			
I can write my school subjects into my timetable in French			
I can write a short description of my school			
I can write a dialogue that gives a short tour of my school			
I can write a blog about my typical day			

Discutez en classe. *Have a class discussion.*

- Look back over your Portfolio exercises. In which areas did you give yourself stars?
- Look at your wishes. Have any of these improved?
- What was your favourite part of Unité 7? Why?
- What did you least enjoy in Unité 7? Why?
- Think about the next unit you will work on. What are you looking forward to learning more about? Why?

UNITÉ 8

Les vacances

By the end of this unit you will

- Say where you are going on holidays and where you are staying
- List the items for your suitcase
- Describe what clothes you will bring on different types of holidays
- Read and understand the signs at the airport
- Go shopping in the airport
- Use the future tense to talk about your holiday plans
- Describe your dream holiday
- Read a postcard about holidays
- Write a postcard to your friend about your holidays
- Read a brochure for a campsite
- Describe a day out at a safari park or an adventure park
- Name animals in French
- Name the amusement rides at an adventure park

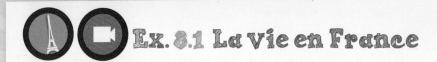

Ex. 8.1 La Vie en France

1. Approximately how many tourists visit France every year?

2. Where can you go skiing in France?

3. What tourist activities are there at the Gorges du Verdon?

4. What surrounds Mont-Saint-Michel?

5. With which queen is Versailles most associated?

6. What made the Concorde different from other planes?

7. How long was Concorde's fastest flight from London to New York?

Objectifs

● I can talk about some popular holiday destinations in France

Visit **http://www.chamonixparc.com/index.php/en/ summer/chamonix-luge-alpine-coster.html** to find out more about the alpine rollercoaster in Chamonix.

Je vais en/au/aux …

When we want to say **to** or **in** for a city or a town, we use à.

● Je vais à Paris.

● Je vais à Navan.

We use *en* for **to** or **in** for a country which is feminine.

● Je vais *en* France.

● Je vais *en* Irlande.

● Je suis *en* Allemagne.

We use *au* for a country which is masculine.

● Je vais *au* Portugal.

We use *aux* for a plural country.

● Je suis *aux* États-Unis.

Ex. 8.2 Vocabulaire

Écoutez le CD et complétez les phrases. *Listen to the CD and fill in the blanks.*

1. Je vais _____ Portugal.

2. Nous allons _____ France.

3. Vous allez _____ Paris.

4. Ils vont _____ Dublin.

5. Elles vont _____ Canada.

6. Tu vas _____ Espagne.

7. Je vais _____ Marseille.

8. Il va _____ Pays-Bas.

9. On va _____ Nice.

10. Je vais _____ Londres.

**Ex. 8.3**

With your partner, think about the grammar rule behind the prepositions *à* and *en*, when we want to say *to* or *in*. *Take turns in explaining and describing this to each other.*

Tu voyages comment pour aller en vacances?
● Je vais en vacances *en* avion.
● Je vais en vacances *en* bateau.
● Je vais en vacances *en* train.
● Je vais en vacances *en* voiture.

Ex. 8.4

Complétez les phrases avec la bonne préposition.

1. Je vais _____ Paris _____ avion.
2. Tu vas _____ Irlande _____ bateau.
3. Il va _____ Dublin _____ train.
4. Elle va _____ Cork _____ voiture.
5. Nous allons _____ France _____ bateau.

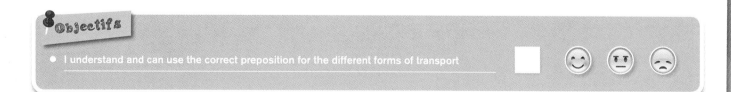

Unité 8 : Les vacances

  Ex. 8.5

Écoutez des jeunes parler de leur vacances. Complétez la grille. *Listen to three young people talking about their holidays. Fill in the grid.*

	Country	Transport
Julie		
Pierre		
Stéphane		

> **Objectifs**
>
> • I can listen and understand when people talk a little about their holiday transport and destination ☺ 😐 ☹

 Ex. 8.6 Infographies

Lisez les infographies et puis répondez aux questions dans votre cahier. *Read the infographics and answer the questions in your copybook.*

(a)

1. What is the most popular holiday accommodation for French people?

2. What are the two least popular forms of accommodation for French people?

3. What is the most popular region of France for French people on holidays?

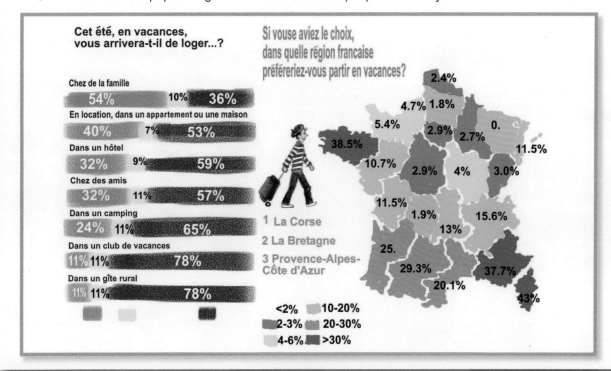

232

(b)

1. What is the most popular activity of French people on holidays?

2. What percentage of French people like to do DIY or gardening during their holidays?

3. What percentage of French people like to play board games on holidays?

4. What is the least popular activity of French people on holidays?

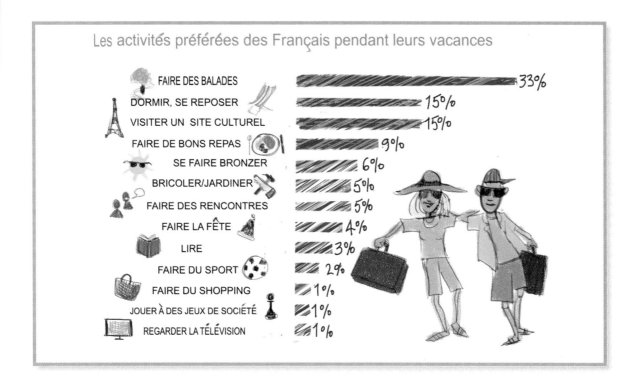

Les activités préférées des Français pendant leurs vacances

Activity	Percentage
FAIRE DES BALADES	33%
DORMIR, SE REPOSER	15%
VISITER UN SITE CULTUREL	15%
FAIRE DE BONS REPAS	9%
SE FAIRE BRONZER	6%
BRICOLER/JARDINER	5%
FAIRE DES RENCONTRES	5%
FAIRE LA FÊTE	4%
LIRE	3%
FAIRE DU SPORT	2%
FAIRE DU SHOPPING	1%
JOUER À DES JEUX DE SOCIÉTÉ	1%
REGARDER LA TÉLÉVISION	1%

Je voudrais …　　　　　*I would like …*

The irregular verb *vouloir* means to wish or to want.

When we want to say what we would like, we use a different tense. We will learn about this tense next year. For now, though, we can use the *je* part of this tense to talk about what we would like.

Je voudrais　　　　　　　　I would like

Je voudrais aller en France.　　I would like to go to France.

The verb after *voudrais* is in the infinitive (the full verb with its ending intact).

- *Je voudrais visiter la tour Eiffel.*

- *Je voudrais boire du café.*

- *Je voudrais voir le film.*

Remember: when we use *je voudrais*, the verb that follows is always in the infinitive.

Ex. 8.7

With your partner, think about the grammar rule behind *je voudrais* **with the infinitive.** *Take turns in explaining and describing this to each other.*

Can you compare the French grammar rule here with how we would say similar phrases in English? Are there similarities? Do other languages in your class use different ways of saying 'I would like'?

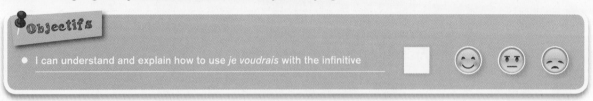

Objectifs

● I can understand and explain how to use *je voudrais* with the infinitive

Ex. 8.8

CD 2 T 52

Écoutez le CD et reliez chaque jeune avec l'image qui correspond. *Listen to the CD and match each description with the correct image.*

Sylvie

Nicolas

Jean

Pierre

Camille

Marine

234

 **Ex. 8.9 À deux**

À deux: posez les questions à votre camarade et répondez à ses questions. **Complétez la grille.** *Talk with your classmate. Ask them questions and reply to theirs. Fill in the grid with your answers and theirs*

Questions	Mes réponses	Les réponses de ma/mon camarade
Tu vas où en vacances ?	Je vais en/au/aux …	
Tu voyages comment pour aller en vacances ?	Je vais en vacances en/par …	
C'est quoi tes vacances de rêves ?	Je voudrais …	

Objectifs

- I can understand when people talk a little about their holiday transport, destination and dream holiday.

- I can use short phrases to answer simple questions about my holiday transport, destination and dream holiday.

 Ex. 8.10 Interévaluation

First, fill in the grid below for yourself, then work with a partner to provide each other with feedback on your performances in Ex. 8.9.

Words I knew really well	
Words I didn't know	
Words I need to pronounce better	
Words I pronounced really well	
My intonation	

Je fais ma valise et je prends …

The verb *faire* is used to form the phrase meaning *to pack your suitcase:*

- *Je fais ma valise.*   I pack my suitcase.

The verb *prendre* means to take.

- *Pour aller en vacances, je fais ma valise et je prends …*

Le verbe *prendre*

Je prends	Elle prend	Vous prenez
Tu prends	On prend	Ils prennent
Il prend	Nous prenons	Elles prennent

Ex. 8.11

With your partner, think about *faire*. *Take turns in answering and explaining these questions:*

1. What is the meaning of the verb *faire*?
2. Is it a regular or an irregular verb?
3. Can you tell your partner three sentences using the verb *faire*?

Objectifs

- I can understand some uses of the verb *faire*

Astuces

Spelling patterns

We have already seen that many English words that end in *y* will have *ie* as their ending in French:

- photography   *la photographie*

English words that end in *ic* often have *ique* as their ending in French.

- picnic   *le pique-nique*

Remember what we learned about cognates in Unit 1? Many of the words for clothes in French are similar to the English versions. Look at the key words in Ex. 8.12 for examples of this.

Ex. 8.12 Vocabulaire

Écoutez le CD et entrainez-vous à bien prononcer le vocabulaire. *Listen to the CD and repeat the vocabulary to improve your pronunciation.*

 Mes vêtements

• un short	• un sweat	• un manteau
• un t-shirt	• un pull	• des chaussettes
• un jean	• un pantalon	• des chaussures
• un survêtement	• une jupe	• des tennis
• un maillot de bain	• une robe	• des baskets
• un chemisier	• une veste	• un chapeau
• un polo	• un blouson	• une casquette

Ex. 8.13 En soldes !

Lisez le texte et répondez aux questions. *Read the text and answer the questions.*

1. How long is the sale on?
2. Can you write the original price of the coat in words in French?

DU 8 JANVIER AU 11 FÉVRIER, JUSQU'À MINUIT

SOLDES

JUSQU'À -60 %

Le manteau
€ 24
€ 60

 Ex. 8.14 Le verbe *prendre*

Décrivez les valises et complétez les phrases avec le verbe *prendre* à la bonne forme. *Describe the contents of the suitcases and fill in the blanks, using the correct part of the verb* prendre.

1. Je fais ma valise. Je _____.

2. Tu fais ta valise. Tu _____.

3. Elle fait sa valise. Elle _____.

4. Nous faisons nos valises. Nous _____.

Objectifs

● I can use the verb *prendre* to describe what I am taking on holidays

Porter

We use the verb *porter* for to wear. *Porter* is a regular –er verb: it takes regular –er endings.

Porter actually has two meanings: to wear and to carry.

Remember the –er verb endings in the present tense?

Je	porte
Tu	portes
Il/Elle/ On	porte
Nous	portons
Vous	portez
Ils/elles	portent

  Ex. 8.15 Le verbe *porter*

Écoutez le CD et complétez les phrases avec le verbe *porter* à la bonne forme. *Listen to the CD and fill in the blanks with the correct part of the verb* porter.

1. Je _____ une robe et des tennis.

2. Il _____ un pantalon, un t-shirt et des baskets.

3. Nous _____ notre uniforme scolaire.

4. Vous _____ une belle jupe.

5. On _____ une chemise bleue.

6. Tu _____ de jolies chaussures.

Ex. 8.16 Que portent-ils?

1. Que porte Marion Cotillard?

2. Que porte Omar Sy?

3. Que porte Audrey Tautou?

Objectifs

- I can use the verb *prendre* to describe what I am taking on holidays

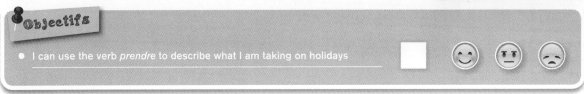

Ex. 8.17

Reliez chaque image avec le mot qui correspond. *Match each image with the correct word.*

un pantalon

une jupe

des baskets

un maillot de bain

un polo

un pull

une robe

Ex. 8.18 Dans ma valise, je prends ...

Vous mettez quels vêtements dans votre valise pour les vacances ci-dessous? *What do you put in your suitcase for the following holidays? Write the lists of clothing below.*

(a)   Je vais en vacances en Suisse. Je fais du ski.
Dans ma valise, je prends …

1. _____des gants_____

2. _____

3. _____

4. _____

5. _____

(b)   Je vais en vacances en Espagne. Je vais au bord de la mer. Dans ma valise, je prends …

1. _____

2. _____

3. _____

4. _____

5. _____

(c)   Je vais en vacances en Irlande. Je vais à Donegal au bord de la mer.
Dans ma valise, je prends …

1. _____

2. _____

3. _____

4. _____

5. _____

Objectifs

● I can describe what clothes to bring on holidays to different destinations _____   ☺ 😠 ☹

  Ex. 8.19 Vocabulaire

Écoutez le CD et entrainez-vous à bien prononcer le vocabulaire. Puis, reliez les images avec les bons mots-clés.
Listen to the CD and repeat the vocabulary to improve your pronunciation. Then match each image with a keyword.

Les affaires indispensables en vacances

- la crème solaire
- ma brosse de dents
- le dentifrice
- ma brosse à cheveux
- le shampooing
- ma serviette
- mes lunettes de soleil
- mon iPod
- un roman
- ma tablette

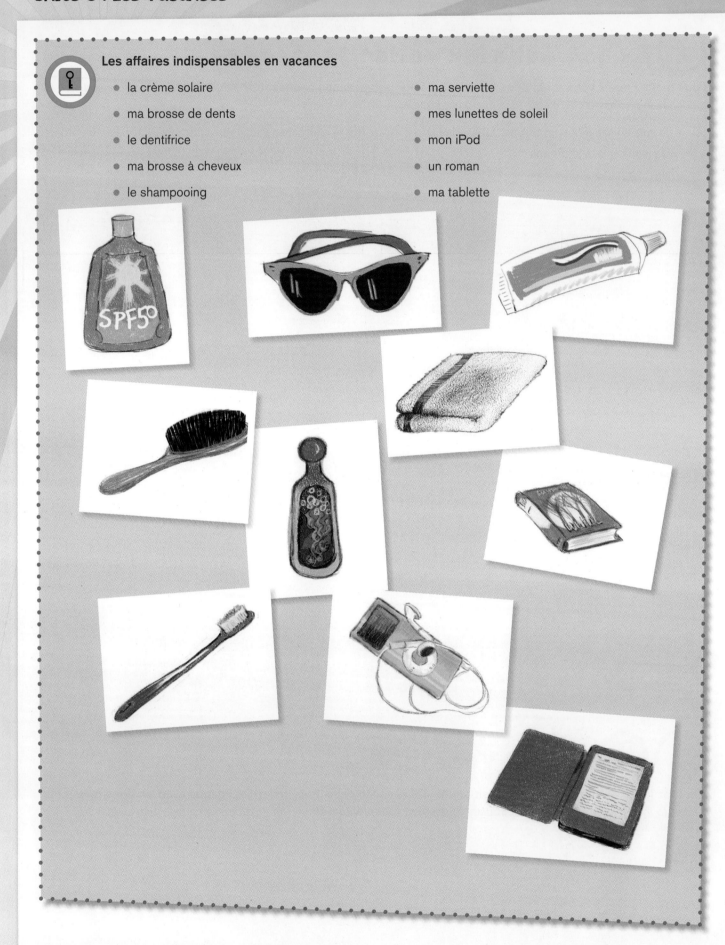

Ex. 8.20 Mots cachés

Traduisez les mots et cherchez-les dans les mots cachés. *Translate the words and find them in the word search.*

Anglais	Français
towel	
sun cream	
shampoo	

Anglais	Français
novel	
toothpaste	
hair brush	

X	L	U	F	T	X	L	M	I	F	R	O	M	A	N
U	D	E	N	T	I	F	R	I	C	E	L	V	V	W
E	J	S	L	L	K	S	O	C	Z	S	Q	E	A	A
V	H	Y	G	C	E	I	C	T	X	G	R	Z	I	T
E	S	E	I	Z	Q	C	B	T	W	I	I	W	Z	M
H	T	H	C	F	I	X	T	Y	A	C	S	U	U	A
C	T	O	A	E	R	V	I	L	N	L	E	W	E	Q
E	O	J	B	M	Z	R	O	U	U	A	R	V	C	V
D	A	J	C	J	P	S	A	N	V	S	V	X	U	X
E	S	O	C	F	E	O	E	Y	K	F	I	H	U	T
S	I	M	B	M	B	T	O	P	I	S	E	R	H	F
S	M	C	È	A	T	F	E	I	N	Q	T	Y	L	L
O	W	R	F	E	W	S	R	J	N	F	T	P	K	D
R	C	Y	S	J	S	X	X	W	F	G	E	U	M	P
B	S	J	U	W	Q	M	C	H	P	G	U	H	K	N

Objectifs

- I can recognise and understand holiday items
- I can read and pronounce holiday items with a French accent

 Ex. 8.21 Dans ma valise, il y a ...

Décrivez les valises. *Describe the contents of the suitcases.*

(a)

(b)

(c)

  Ex. 8.22 Vocabulaire

Écoutez le CD et entrainez-vous à bien prononcer le vocabulaire. *Listen to the CD and repeat the vocabulary to improve your pronunciation.*

 A l'aéroport – Les panneaux

- ARRIVÉES
- DÉPARTS
- PHARMACIE

- PRESSE
- TOILETTES
- CONSIGNE

- LOCATION DE VOITURE
- PARKING

 Ex. 8.23

Répondez aux questions avec votre camarade. *Answer the questions with your partner, using the mots-clés from p.244.*

1. Which sign do you follow if you want to buy a newspaper?
2. Which sign do you follow if you want to hire a car?
3. Which sign do you follow if you want to park your car?
4. Which sign do you follow if you want to go the chemist?
5. Which sign do you follow if you are going to Departures to catch your flight?
6. Which sign do you follow if you need to use the bathroom?
7. Which sign do you follow if you are collecting someone from Arrivals?
8. Which sign do you follow if you want to use an airport locker?

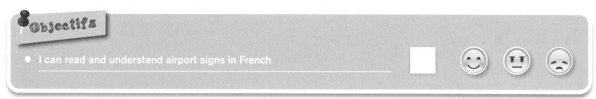
Objectifs
● I can read and understand airport signs in French

 Ex. 8.24

Lisez les scènes et répondez aux questions dans votre cahier. *Read the scenes and answer the questions in your copybook.*

Amélie :	Je suis super contente d'aller en vacances avec toi, Mélanie ! J'ai hâte d'être à l'appartement !
Mélanie :	Oui, moi aussi, Amélie. L'appartement sera super. Ah j'adore les vacances ! Au fait, j'ai besoin de nouvelles lunettes de soleil, et aussi de crème solaire.
Amélie :	Ah oui ? Alors, on va à la pharmacie ?
Mélanie :	Oui, s'il te plait. Où est la pharmacie ?
Amélie :	Regarde, c'est là-bas !
	À la pharmacie
Mélanie :	J'aime bien ces lunettes-là. Amélie, comment tu les trouves ?
Amélie :	Moi, je n'aime pas la couleur, je préfère les lunettes noires.
Mélanie :	Tu as raison, les lunettes noires sont plus jolies.
Amélie :	N'oublie pas la crème solaire !
Mélanie :	Ah oui, merci. On prend de la crème indice de protection 30?
Amélie :	Oui, voilà.
	À la caisse
Le vendeur :	Bonjour.
Mélanie :	Bonjour, je prends les lunettes de soleil et la crème solaire, s'il vous plait.
Le vendeur :	Ça fait 45 euros, s'il vous plait.
Mélanie :	Voilà 50 euros.
Le vendeur :	Et voici votre monnaie. Bonne journée !
Mélanie :	Bonne journée, au revoir.

1. What does Mélanie think of their holiday apartment?
2. What does she need to buy at the pharmacy?
3. What colour does Amélie recommend for the sunglasses?
4. How much does Mélanie spend?

5. Translate:

I am very happy	
I can't wait	
I need	
prettier	
over there	
Have a nice day	

6. Act out the scene with your classmates.

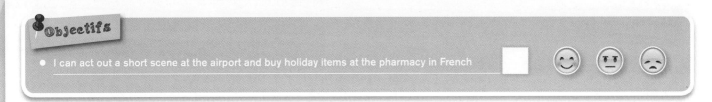

Objectifs

- I can act out a short scene at the airport and buy holiday items at the pharmacy in French

Ex. 8.25 Vocabulaire

Écoutez le CD et entrainez-vous à bien prononcer le vocabulaire. *Listen to the CD and repeat the vocabulary to improve your pronunciation.*

Shopping à l'aéroport

- Je voudrais …
- Ça fait combien ?

- Ça fait …
- Voici votre monnaie.
- Bonne journée !

Ex. 8.26 Qu'est-ce que les jeunes achètent ?

Écoutez les conversations. Complétez la grille. *Listen to the conversations and fill in the grid.*

	What do they buy?	How much does it cost altogether?
Jean		
Pierre		
Jake		

Mon portfolio 8.1 : Un jeu de rôle.

Faites exercice dans votre portfolio. *Do this exercise in your portfolio.*

  Ex. 8.27 Vocabulaire

Écoutez le CD et entrainez-vous à bien prononcer le vocabulaire. *Listen to the CD and repeat the vocabulary to improve your pronunciation.*

Tu vas où ?
- Je vais/je suis en vacances …
- à la plage
- à la campagne
- au bord de la mer
- à la montagne
- près d'un lac
- dans une station balnéaire
- dans un camping

Tu loges où ?
- dans un hôtel
- dans une auberge de jeunesse
- une chambre d'hôte
- dans une tente
- dans un mobil-home
- dans un camping-car

 Ex. 8.28

Regardez les images et décrivez les lieux et les logements.

Objectifs

- I can recognise and understand keywords about holiday locations and accommodation

Astuces

Use these tips for **listening** exercises.

- If there is any text to accompany the listening exercise, read the text carefully and think about the topic before you listen. Try to identify any keywords you should listen out for.

- Don't panic if you don't understand every word! Try to work out the general meaning by focusing on words you do recognise: nouns, adjectives and verbs will always provide useful clues.

- Listen more than once – ideally, three or four times. Your ear will tune into the piece and you will decipher more words and sounds each time you listen.

- Even if you can answer all the questions that accompany a piece, it is a good idea to listen to the piece again anyway. You might pick up extra words and phrases to use another time.

CD 2 T 62

Ex. 8.29

Écoutez des jeunes parler de leurs vacances. Complétez la grille. *Listen to the CD and fill in the table.*

	How are they travelling?	What country are they going to?	Where are they holidaying?	What accommodation are they staying in?
Bertrand				
David				
Florent				

Objectifs

- I can understand when people talk a little about their holiday transport, destination and accommodation, using simple sentences

France is full of wonderful holiday destinations. Off the south coast of France is a small group of islands where there are no cars – only bicycles. Research *Île de Porquerolles* to find out more!

Ex. 8.30 Les cartes postales

Lisez les carte postales et répondez aux questions. *Read the postcards and answer the questions.*

(a)

Chère Siobhan,

Me voici en vacances à La Rochelle, en France. Ici, il fait beau et chaud. La plage est belle et je joue au volley tous les jours. J'aime bien nager dans la mer. La Rochelle est une très belle ville. Nous logeons dans un camping au bord de la mer. Notre tente est confortable. Le camping est bien équipé : il y a une belle piscine et des terrains de sport. Il y a beaucoup de choses à faire et à voir ici. J'aime la cuisine française, surtout les baguettes et les croissants !

À bientôt,

Marie-Laure

(b)

Cher James,

Salutations de Bordeaux ! Ici, il fait chaud mais il pleut. La ville de Bordeaux est très grande et très belle. J'aime le grand théâtre et j'adore la cuisine ici. Nous logeons dans un hôtel. Notre chambre est très confortable avec une belle vue sur la ville. Maman aime visiter les vignobles et gouter le vin ! Papa aime surtout les gâteaux !

À bientôt,

Luc

1. Where is Luc on holidays and where is he staying?

2. Where is Marie-Laure on holidays and where is she staying?

3. What view does Luc have?

4. How does Marie-Laure describe the weather?

(c) **Trouvez les paires.** *Find the pairs.*

Me voici	dans un camping.
Il fait beau	de Bordeaux
Nous logeons	il pleut.
Salutations	très confortable.
Il fait chaud mais	en vacances.
Notre chambre est	et chaud.

(d) **Traduisez.** *Translate*

Anglais	Français		Anglais	Français
The beach is nice			especially	
every day			very comfortable	
by the sea			a nice view of the city	
There's lots to see and do			vineyards	

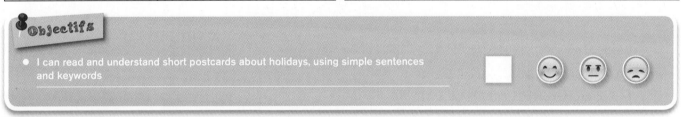

Objectifs

- I can read and understand short postcards about holidays, using simple sentences and keywords

Ex. 8.31 Vocabulaire

Écoutez le CD et entrainez-vous à bien prononcer le vocabulaire. *Listen to the CD and repeat the vocabulary to improve your pronunciation.*

Une carte postale

- Me voici …
- Salutations de …
- Il fait beau/chaud.
- Il y a du soleil.
- Il pleut.
- J'aime bien…
- Je fais …
- Je loge …/nous logeons …
- À bientôt !

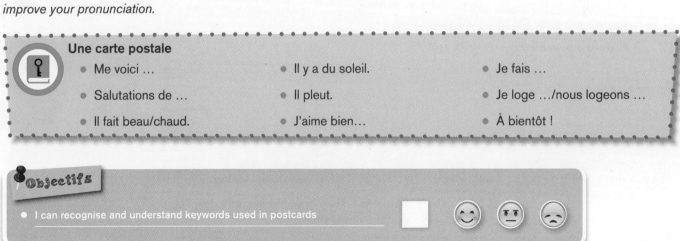

Objectifs

- I can recognise and understand keywords used in postcards

Mon portfolio 8.2 : Ma carte postale

Fais cet exercice dans ton portfolio. *Do this exercise in your portfolio.*

Ex. 8.32 La vie en France

Regardez la vidéo et répondez aux questions. *Watch the video and answer the questions.*

1. Approximately how many campsites are there in France?

2. Name two types of accommodation you can stay in.

3. Name two facilities in French campsites.

4. Name one campsite beside the sea and one campsite beside a *château*.

Ex. 8.33 Vocabulaire

Écoutez le CD et entrainez-vous à bien prononcer le vocabulaire. *Listen to the CD and repeat the vocabulary to improve your pronunciation.*

Au terrain du camping

- un terrain de camping
- une tente
- un mobil-home
- un camping-car

- un emplacement
- une caravane
- une aire de jeux
- un barbecue
- un restaurant

- une laverie
- un magasin
- un mini-club pour les jeunes
- la salle de jeux

- les douches
- le tri des ordures
- la réception

Astuces

The last consonant of French words is usually not pronounced. But some such as *c, r, f,* and *l* are pronounced. So be **CaReFuL**!

Remember that when *e* appears at the end of a noun, this often allows us to pronounce the consonant that comes just before the *e*. Examples:

- We **do** pronounce the *t* at the end of *une ten**te***.

- We **do not** pronounce the *t* at the end of *un emplacemen**t***.

Objectifs

- I can read, listen and understand keywords for campsites in French

 Visit http://www.les-castels.com to see some French campsites.

Ex. 8.34 Mots cachés

Traduisez les mots et cherchez-les dans les mots cachés. *Translate the words and find them in the word search.*

Anglais	Français
tent	
laundry	
showers	
shop	
caravan	

N	Y	V	D	H	N	X	G	D	L	T	I	S	Z	U
T	I	H	A	U	A	W	U	A	H	S	Z	B	B	H
Y	H	S	Z	S	V	C	V	A	P	C	H	E	Z	K
G	Z	W	A	G	A	E	S	E	H	C	U	O	D	K
Q	T	E	A	G	R	Y	Q	K	E	F	Y	L	C	I
F	A	P	K	I	A	L	Z	W	J	G	S	P	Y	U
S	Z	U	E	H	C	M	K	P	B	O	I	T	C	C
F	X	G	Y	W	R	H	I	S	K	P	E	B	Y	E
Z	L	T	H	B	Z	A	Z	V	M	G	F	M	J	A
W	Z	A	A	K	A	I	H	H	E	M	P	S	L	D
Q	V	T	N	Y	W	E	Z	T	K	X	Y	G	D	M
Z	V	M	K	Q	C	K	N	P	M	K	A	N	V	J
K	P	W	Q	V	B	E	N	Q	X	X	M	Y	D	C
C	J	A	H	H	T	V	V	J	U	F	B	P	L	L
B	W	G	W	U	C	A	R	A	V	A	N	E	X	C

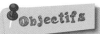
  Ex. 8.35

Écoutez des gens parler de leur terrain de camping idéal. Trouvez les images qui correspondent. *People talk about their choices for campsites. Listen to the CD and match the images.*

Claudette

J'ai trois enfants, et pour moi, une aire de jeux est indispensable. Nous voulons loger dans un mobil-home. Je voudrais aussi pouvoir manger dans un restaurant, dans le camping.

Louise

J'adore nager et jouer au foot. Je voudrais trouver un camping avec un café.

Pierre

Pour moi, le recyclage, c'est très important. J'achète aussi beaucoup de produits bio. J'adore faire du camping dans une tente.

David

J'adore aller à la campagne parce que j'aime bien aller à la pêche. Je voudrais loger dans une tente, dans un camping près d'un lac. Je voudrais aussi louer un vélo.

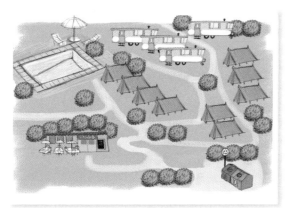 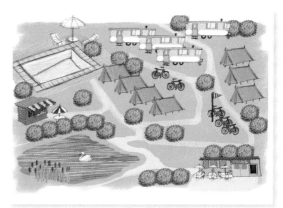

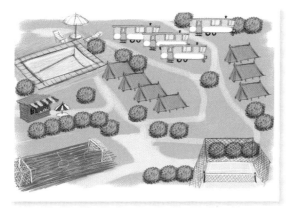 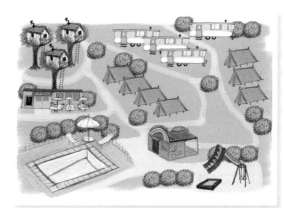

Unité 8 : Les vacances

Le futur proche

We use this tense when we are talking about the near future. Examples:

● I am going to go to France. ● I am going to travel by plane.

These sentences are in *le futur proche*. It is easy to form:

Step 1: Use the present tense of *aller*.

Je **vais**
Tu **vas**
Il/Elle/On **va**
Nous **allons**
Vous **allez**
Ils/Elles **vont**

Step 2: Add the infinitive.

Examples:

● I am going to visit Paris.

*Je vais **visiter** Paris.*

● I am going to buy a present.

*Je vais **acheter** un cadeau.*

● We are going to watch TV.

*Nous allons **regarder** la télé.*

 Ex. 8.36 Le futur proche

Écrivez les phrases au futur proche. *Write these sentences in* le futur proche.

1. Je ___vais___ (aller) ___visiter___ (visiter) Paris cet été avec ma famille.

2. Nous _____ (aller) _____ (manger) dans de grands restaurants.

3. Ils _____ (aller) _____ (aller) à Disneyland Paris pour une journée exceptionnelle.

4. Elle _____ (aller) _____ (voyager) de Dublin à Paris en avion.

5. Nous _____ (aller) _____ (loger) dans un camping très confortable à la campagne.

254

Ex. 8.37 Le blog de Noah

Écoutez la CD et répondez aux questions. *Listen to the CD and answer the questions.*

(a) **Complétez le texte.** *Fill in the blanks.*

Je suis _____ parce que c'est les vacances ! Deux mois de liberté !

Cette année, pendant les vacances, ma famille et moi _____ passer

deux semaines dans le sud de la France, à Fréjus. Je _____ mon

_____, mes shorts, mes t-shirts, mes _____,

de la crème solaire et mes tongs parce que nous _____ dans un camping

au bord de la mer. Nous _____ dans un mobil-home avec trois chambres. Je

_____ avec mon frère dans une des chambres.

Le terrain de camping est _____, c'est un camping 5 étoiles. Il est super bien

équipé : il y a _____, un restaurant, _____, une

aire de jeux pour les enfants, des magasins, des terrains de tennis, un terrain de basket et un terrain de foot. Il est

juste _____ la mer.

Je _____ dans la piscine et je _____ au tennis

avec mon frère. Ma mère _____ dans la mer et elle va faire des promenades.

Nous _____ une journée dans un parc animalier. J'adore les animaux et

je _____ des tigres, des _____ et des

_____. J'ai hâte d'être en vacances !

(b) **Trouvez quatre exemples du futur proche.** *Find four examples of* le futur proche. *Write them in the grid and translate them into English.*

(c)

1. Where is Fréjus?
2. Name three items Noah is going to bring on holidays.
3. What accommodation will he stay in?
4. Name two facilities on the campsite.
5. Name one thing Noah will do on his holidays.
6. Name one thing his mother will do on her holidays.
7. Where will they also spend the day on holidays?
8. What will he see there?

Unité 8 : Les vacances

Objectifs

- I can listen to and understand a blog about holiday plans in *le futur proche*

😊 😐 ☹️

Ex. 8.38 Mes projets de vacances

(a) **Regardez les images et décrivez vos projets avec les verbes suivants au futur proche.** *Look at the images and describe your holiday plans, using the verbs below in* la futur proche.

aller　　　　nager　　　　regarder　　　　loger　　　　jouer　　　　acheter

(b) **À deux: posez les questions à votre camarade et répondez à ses questions. Complétez la grille.**
Talk with your classmate. Ask them questions and reply to theirs. Fill in the grid with your answers and theirs.

Questions	Mes réponses	Les réponses de ma/ mon camarade
Tu vas où en vacances ?		
Tu vas en vacances avec qui ?		
Qu'est-ce que tu vas faire ?		
Tu vas loger où ?		

Ex. 8.39 Interévaluation

First, fill in the grid below for yourself, then work with a partner to provide each other with feedback on your performances in Ex. 8.38.

Words I knew really well	
Words I didn't know	
Words I need to pronounce better	
Words I pronounced really well	
My intonation	

Ex. 8.40 Vocabulaire

Écoutez le CD et entrainez-vous à bien prononcer le vocabulaire. Puis, reliez les images avec les bons mots-clés.
Listen to the CD and repeat the vocabulary to improve your pronunciation. Then match each image with a keyword.

Les animaux du parc animalier

- un tigre
- un lion
- un ours
- un ours polaire
- un crocodile
- un singe
- un kangourou
- un pingouin
- un zèbre
- un éléphant
- une girafe

Objectifs

- I can read, understand and recognise names of animals in French

  ### Ex. 8.41 Une visite au parc animalier

Écoutez le CD et répondez aux questions. *Listen to the CD and answer the questions.*

(a) **Remplissez les blancs.** *Fill in the blanks.*

Nous sommes en vacances, près de Royan, _____ l'ouest de la France.

Vendredi, nous _____ le parc zoologique de la Palmyre, c'est tout près.

Maman et moi, on adore les animaux, surtout les _____. Je n'ai pas peur

des lions : ils sont féroces mais tellement beaux ! À la Palmyre, on _____

beaucoup d'animaux différents : de très grandes _____, des

_____ assez méchants et de vieux _____ .

On _____ au parc en voiture, et à midi, s'il fait beau,

on _____. Ça va être génial, on va bien s'amuser !

_____ à vendredi !

(b)

1. Where is Noah on holiday?
2. Where is the safari park?
3. What animal does Noah especially like? Why?
4. Who is he going to visit the park with?
5. What will they do if the weather holds out?

● I can read and understand a short blog about a visit to a safari park, using *le futur proche*

 Ex. 8.42

Reliez chaque animal avec son cri ! *Match the animals to the correct sounds!*

Groin-groin

Cocorico

Piou-piou

Hi-han

Coin-coin

Meuh

Miaou

Ouaf ouaf

 Visit www.safari-peaugres.com to learn about a safari park in **Auvergne-Rhône-Alpes**. What animals live in the safari park? How much does it cost to visit the safari park?

Unité 8 : Les vacances

 ## Ex. 8.43 À mon avis ...

Work with your partner to revise the vocabulary we learned for the
Group Talks in *Unité 1* and *Unité 5* (see page 20).
Now use the images on the right to do a Group Talk.

 ### Astuces

See page 21 for a reminder on how a Group Talk works!

Objectifs

- I can participate in Group Talk

  ## Ex. 8.44 Vocabulaire

Écoutez le CD et entrainez-vous à bien prononcer le vocabulaire. Puis, reliez les images avec les bons mots-clés.
Listen to the CD and repeat the vocabulary to improve your pronunciation. Then match each image with a keywords.

Une journée dans un parc d'attractions

- le toboggan géant
- les autos tamponneuses
- les chaises volantes
- le manège
- le bateau pirate

- le petit train
- le château
- le labyrinthe
- la rivière enchantée
- un billet

- l'entrée
- l'hôtel
- les magasins de souvenirs

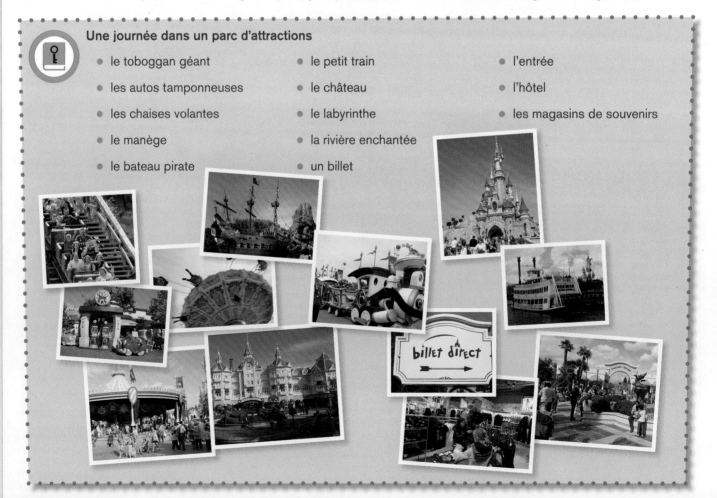

  Ex. 8.45 Mes projets pour les grandes vacances

Écoutez le CD et complétez les textes. *Listen to the CD and fill in the blanks.*

Céline

Moi, cet été, je _____ en vacances à Paris avec ma famille. Je

_____ dans un hôtel à Disneyland Paris. Nous _____

là-bas pendant une semaine. Je _____ dans la piscine de l'hôtel et je

_____ dans les restaurants du parc. Et bien sur,

je _____ toutes les attractions, surtout les autos tamponneuses et les chaises volantes.

Les chaises volantes, c'est mon attraction préférée. Le dernier jour, je _____ des

cadeaux pour mes amis dans les magasins de souvenirs.

Jérôme

Pendant les grandes vacances, je _____ à Paris avec ma famille. Nous

_____ là-bas pendant deux semaines. Nous _____

dans un appartement au centre-ville. Nous _____ dans de bons restaurants

tous les soirs ! Je _____ la tour Eiffel, le musée du Louvre et le Sacré-

Cœur. Je _____ aux Galeries Lafayette pour acheter des cadeaux. Nous

_____ de super bonnes vacances, j'ai hâte !

Laetitia

Cet été, pendant les grandes vacances, je _____ à Saint-Malo avec ma famille.

On _____ pendant trois semaines. On _____ dans un

gite au bord de la mer. Je _____ le Mont Saint-Michel et les iles Chausey et je

_____ des crêpes et du camembert, j'adore ça ! J'ai vraiment hâte d'être en vacances !

 **Mon portfolio 8.3 : Mon blog sur les grandes vacances**

Faites cet exercice dans votre portfolio. *Do this exercise in your portfolio.*

Mots-clés pour l'Unité 8

Le verbe *prendre*

Je prends	Elle prend	Vous prenez
Tu prends	On prend	Ils prennent
Il prend	Nous prenons	Elles prennent

Mes vetements

- un short
- un t-shirt
- un jean
- un survêtement
- un maillot de bain
- un chemisier
- un polo

- un sweat
- un pull
- un pantalon
- une jupe
- une robe
- une veste
- un blouson

- un manteau
- des chaussettes
- des chaussures
- des tennis
- des baskets
- un chapeau
- une casquette

Les affaires indispensables en vacances

- la crème solaire
- ma brosse de dents
- le dentifrice
- ma brosse à cheveux

- le shampooing
- ma serviette
- mes lunettes de soleil
- mon iPod

- un roman
- ma tablette

À l'aéroport – les panneaux

- ARRIVÉES
- DÉPARTS
- PHARMACIE

- PRESSE
- TOILETTES
- CONSIGNE

- LOCATION DE VOITURE
- PARKING

Shopping à l'aéroport

- Je voudrais …
- Ça fait combien ?

- Ça fait …
- Voici votre monnaie.

- Bonne journée !

Tu vas où ?

- Je vais/je suis en vacances …
- à la plage

- à la campagne
- au bord de la mer
- à la montagne

- près d'un lac
- dans une station balnéaire
- dans un camping

Tu loges où ?

- dans un hôtel
- dans une auberge de jeunesse

- une chambre d'hôte
- dans une tente
- dans un mobil-home

- dans un camping-car

Une carte postale

- Me voici …
- Salutations de …
- Il fait beau/chaud.
- Il y a du soleil.
- Il pleut.
- J'aime bien…
- Je fais …
- Je loge …/nous logeons …
- À bientôt !

Au terrain de camping

- un terrain de camping
- une tente
- un mobil-home
- un camping-car
- un emplacement
- une caravane
- une aire de jeux
- un barbecue
- un restaurant
- une laverie
- un magasin
- un mini-club pour les jeunes
- la salle de jeux
- les douches
- le tri des ordures
- la réception

Les animaux du parc animalier

- un tigre
- un lion
- un ours
- un ours polaire
- un crocodile
- un singe
- un kangourou
- un pingouin
- un zèbre
- un éléphant
- une girafe

Une journée dans un parc d'attraction

- le toboggan géant
- les autos tamponneuses
- les chaises volantes
- le manège
- le bateau pirate
- le petit train
- le château
- le labyrinthe
- la rivière enchantée
- un billet
- l'entrée
- l'hôtel
- les magasins de souvenirs

Unité 8 : Les vacances

Bilan de l'Unité 8. *Checklist for Unit 8.*

Pour chaque objectif, choisissez votre émoticône.	🙂	😐	🙁
Listening			
I can understand when someone says where they are going and where they will stay on their holidays			
I can understand when someone describes how they travel			
I can understand when someone describes their dream holiday			
I can understand when someone describes what they will bring on holidays			
I can understand when someone describes what they are wearing			
I can understand short conversations at the airport			
I can understand when I hear someone shopping at the pharmacy			
I can understand when I hear people talking about a campsite			
I can understand when I hear people talking about their holiday plans			
I can understand when I hear a blog about a holiday at a campsite			
I can understand when I hear someone talking about a trip to an adventure park			
Reading			
I can read short infographics about holidays in France			
I can read a list of clothes and holiday items for packing			
I can read a short scene about going on holidays and shopping at the airport			
I can read signs at the airport			
I can read a blog about future holiday plans			
I can read a blog about holidays, a trip to a safari park and a day out at an adventure park			
Spoken production			
I can talk about some popular holiday destinations in France			
I can say where I am going and where I am staying on my holidays			
I can describe my dream holiday, using simple sentences			

I can name clothes in French			
I can list what clothes and items I will take on holidays			
I can name places in the airport			
I can name facilities at a campsite			
I can talk about my holiday plans			
I can describe a day at the safari park, using simple phrases			
I can name animals in French			
I can describe a day at the adventure park, using simple sentences			
I can name the amusement rides in French			
Spoken interaction			
I can ask someone where they are going and where they are staying on their holidays			
I can ask someone about their holiday plans			
I can shop at the airport			
I can answer questions about my holidays and plans			
Writing			
I can write a blog about my holidays and my holiday plans			
I can write a postcard about my holidays and holiday plans			
I can use *le futur proche* to write about my holiday plans			
I can write a role play to buy holiday items			
I can label facilities at the airport, a campsite and amusement rides at a theme park			

Discutez en classe. *Have a class discussion.*

- Look back over your Portfolio exercises. In which areas did you give yourself stars?

- Look at your wishes. Have any of these improved?

- What was your favourite part of Unité 8? Why?

- What did you least enjoy in Unité 8? Why?

- Thinking back over all the units, which one did you most enjoy? Why?

1. **Lisez la lettre et répondez aux questions dans votre cahier.** *Read the letter and answer the questions in your copybook.*

Sarlat, le 17 juillet

Cher Seamus,

Merci pour ta dernière lettre que j'ai reçue il y a une semaine. Tu m'as demandé de te parler un peu de Sarlat et ma maison. La ville de Sarlat est très belle. Elle se trouve en Dordogne, une région très pittoresque et historique dans le sud-est de la France, pas trop loin de Bordeaux. Notre maison est petite, vieille mais très confortable avec un joli jardin à côté d'une rivière. Il y a trois chambres, une petite cuisine, une salle à manger, un salon et trois salles de bains. Dans le jardin il y a une belle piscine – je l'adore surtout pendant l'été quand il fait chaud !

La Dordogne est pleine de vieux châteaux et de vieux villages comme le village de Domme. Domme se situe pas trop loin de chez moi. En été les touristes prennent le petit train pour voir le village. Il est mignon ! Le marché de Domme a lieu chaque jeudi et il y a beaucoup de légumes et fruits frais, des jolies fleurs et des souvenirs.

Veux-tu nous rendre visite pendant les vacances de la Toussaint ? Nous pourrons visiter Domme et Sarlat. Nous pouvons aussi aller au cinéma et sortir avec mes amis. Laisse-moi savoir si tu pourras venir.

À bientôt !

Julie

1. When did Julie get the letter from Seamus?
2. What did Seamus ask her to write about?
3. Where in France is Sarlat?
4. Give three details about Julie's house.
5. What is Domme?
6. What do the tourists do there in the summer?
7. What can you buy in the market?
8. When does the market take place?
9. Julie invites Seamus to her home for what time of year?
10. Name one thing that Julie says they can do.

2. **Faites des recherches sur Internet, puis répondez aux questions dans votre cahier.** *Research online, then answer the questions in your copybook.*

1. Canada is a francophone country. In what province in Canada is French spoken as a first language?

2. What is the capital of this province?

3. Find out three things about a famous winter festival held in this French-speaking province of Canada.

4. What are the official languages of Canada?

5. Name a famous singer from this part of Canada.

3. **Écrivez les phrases au futur proche.** *Write these sentences in* le futur proche.

1. Nous _____ (aller) _____ (voyager) en France cet été en bateau.

2. Je _____ (aller) _____ (voir) le film ce soir.

3. Il _____ (aller) _____ (visiter) Paris pendant son séjour en France.

4. Elles _____ (aller) _____ (faire) un gâteau au chocolat pour leur amie.

5. Tu _____ (aller) _____ (loger) dans un hôtel de luxe au bord de la mer.

4. **Écrivez une carte postale à votre ami(e).** *Write a postcard to your friend.*

- You are on holidays with your family in France for two weeks.
- The weather is hot and sunny.
- You are staying in a campsite.
- Tomorrow you are going to visit a theme park

5. Jeu de plateau. *Board game.*

You will need:

- A different coloured counter for each player
- A dice

Rules

- 2–5 players
- The youngest player rolls first, the second-youngest rolls second, etc.
- Roll the dice and move on that number of squares.
- Take the challenge on your square.
- If you give an incorrect answer, you miss a turn.
- The first player to reach 'Vous avez gagné' wins the game!

Astuces

Try to use as much French as possible during the game. Here are some useful phrases.

Commençons !	Let's begin!
À moi !	My turn!
À toi !	Your turn!
Lance le dé !	Throw the dice!
Avance d'une case !	Move forward one square!
Recule d'une case !	Go back one square!

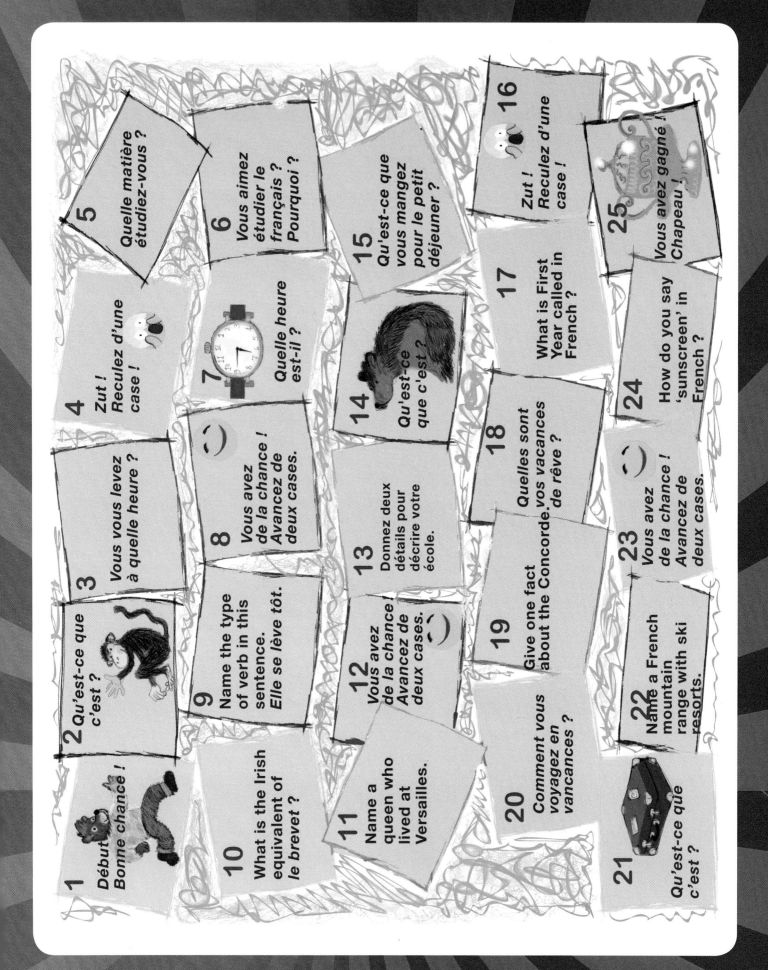

1 Début ! Bonne chance !

2 Qu'est-ce que c'est ?

3 Vous vous levez à quelle heure ?

4 Zut ! Reculez d'une case !

5 Quelle matière étudiez-vous ?

6 Vous aimez étudier le français ? Pourquoi ?

7 Quelle heure est-il ?

8 Vous avez de la chance ! Avancez de deux cases.

9 Name the type of verb in this sentence. Elle se lève tôt.

10 What is the Irish equivalent of le brevet ?

11 Name a queen who lived at Versailles.

12 Vous avez de la chance ! Avancez de deux cases.

13 Donnez deux détails pour décrire votre école.

14 Qu'est-ce que c'est ?

15 Qu'est-ce que vous mangez pour le petit déjeuner ?

16 Zut ! Reculez d'une case !

17 What is First Year called in French ?

18 Quelles sont vos vacances de rêve ?

19 Give one fact about the Concorde.

20 Comment vous voyagez en vancances ?

21 Qu'est-ce que c'est ?

22 Name a French mountain range with ski resorts.

23 Vous avez de la chance ! Avancez de deux cases.

24 How do you say 'sunscreen' in French ?

25 Vous avez gagné ! Chapeau !

6. **Une petite pièce de théâtre !** *A little piece of theatre play!*

Below is the script for a short play. Act it out in small groups. It's a great way to practise your new vocabulary. Audience members can take notes to help the actors improve on their pronunciation!

Présentation

La famille Mounier va en vacances. Ils sont à l'aéroport. Ils parlent de leurs projets pour les vacances en France.

Liste des personnages

- Monsieur Mounier
- Madame Mounier
- Jamie
- Lola

Lola : J'ai hâte d'aller en vacances Maman !

Madame Mounier :

Oui, moi aussi, chérie. Alors, je voudrais acheter de la crème solaire.

[Elle va à la pharmacie].

Jamie : Papa, tu voudrais aller au parc d'attractions ? Moi, je voudrais aller au zoo et au parc d'attractions !

Monsieur Mounier :

Oui, moi aussi. J'ai hâte de faire le toboggan géant !

Lola : Mais non, ce n'est pas mon truc, Papa. Je vais aller à la piscine.

[Madame Mounier revient avec sa crème solaire].

Madame Mounier :

Nous avons tous des projets pour les vacances. Moi je voudrais visiter le musée, et faire des promenades sur la plage.

Monsieur Mounier :

Je suis d'accord, je voudrais visiter le musée aussi.

Lola et Jamie :

Ah non, pas nous ! C'est trop nul, les musées !

Madame Mounier :

Allez vite ! C'est l'heure du départ. L'avion va partir sans nous, dépêchez-vous !

270

Les verbes réguliers

ER **IR** **RE**

Regarder : To look

Je regarde
Tu regardes
Il/elle/on regarde
Nous regardons
Vous regardez
Ils/elles regardent

Finir : To finish

Je finis
Tu finis
Il/elle/on finit
Nous finissons
Vous finissez
Ils/elles finissent

Vendre : To sell

Je vends
Tu vends
Il/elle/on vend
Nous vendons
Vous vendez
Ils/elles vendent

Les verbes irréguliers

Être : To be

Je suis
Tu es
Il/elle/on est
Nous sommes
Vous êtes
Ils/elles sont

Avoir : To have

J'ai
Tu as
Il/elle/on a
Nous avons
Vous avez
Ils/elles ont

Faire : To make/To do

Je fais
Tu fais
Il/elle/on fait
Nous faisons
Vous faites
Ils/elles font

Aller : To go

Je vais
Tu vas
Il/elle/on va
Nous allons
Vous allez
Ils/elles vont

Manger : To eat

Je mange
Tu manges
Il/elle/on mange
Nous mangeons
Vous mangez
Ils/elles mangent

Boire : To drink

Je bois
Tu bois
Il/elle/on boit
Nous buvons
Vous buvez
Ils/elles boivent

Les verbes

Se lever: To get up	**Se laver : To wash (oneself)**	**Prendre : To take**
Je me lève	Je me lave	Je prends
Tu te lèves	Tu te laves	Tu prends
Il/elle/on se lève	Il/elle/on se lave	Il/elle/on prend
Nous nous levons	Nous nous lavons	Nous prenons
Vous vous levez	Vous vous lavez	Vous prenez
Ils/elles se lèvent	Ils/elles se lavent	Ils/elles prennent